Successful Prosecution of Intim:

Offender-focused prosecution concentrates attention to the actions, decisions, choices, and motivations of the offender. Crimes of intimate violence tend to compel investigators, prosecutors, and defense attorneys to fixate on the victim's behavior to prove or disprove a case. Prosecutors can become helpless when faced with uncooperative victims, challenging facts, or attacks on the victims' credibility. However, when the prosecution can rely on evidence and offender-focused interviewing, investigation, and case construction, there is a greater chance of success.

This book will offer investigators and prosecutors concrete information and techniques to construct and present offender-focused cases in crimes of intimate violence. First, we will challenge the reader's biases and assumptions about intimate violence, providing information that will dispel pervasive myths and misinformation we maintain. We will explain the motivations and techniques that offenders use on their victims to ensure the victims' silence, compliance, and resistance to prosecution. The second section will address specific steps that investigators and prosecutors can take for offender-focused prosecution, including interviewing practices, conducting evidence-based investigations, selecting and preparing a jury, and building an offender-focused prosecution through the case. The reader will be offered practical and attainable practices and skills.

This book will be primarily intended for investigators or prosecutors. However, it will be accessible to paralegals, victim advocates, judges, and others involved in the criminal justice system to utilize.

Bridget H. Ryan is a Special Victim Litigation Expert (SVLE) assigned to the Trial Counsel Assistance Program of the United States Army Legal Services Agency. In her capacity, she provides curriculum development, training, and technical assistance to trial counsel on sexual assault, domestic violence, and child abuse cases, assisting the trial team at court's martials around the globe. She received her J.D. from the University of Illinois Chicago John Marshall Law School. Prior to 2009, Ms. Ryan was the Director of Legal Hiring and Recruiting, Director of Public Affairs, and the Violence Against Women Policy Advisor for the Cook County State's Attorney's Office, advising the State's Attorney of the nation's second-largest prosecuting office on domestic violence and sexual assault. Ms. Ryan developed and presented training sessions on domestic violence and sexual assault to multidisciplinary audiences. She has been Faculty of the National College of District Attorneys, the National District Attorney's Association, The American Prosecutors Research Institute, the Department of Homeland Security's Federal Law Enforcement Training Center, the National Sheriff's Association, and the International Association of Forensic Nurses. Ms. Ryan was nominated for an Emmy as a co-producer of "Not in My School," a video educating youth on the effects of hate crimes. She was named one of Illinois "Top 40 Lawyers under 40" and chosen to do a fellowship in Leadership Greater Chicago, which identifies leadership in the Chicago area, having famous alumni such as Michelle Obama, Arne Duncan, and Austan Goolsbee.

Veronique N. Valliere is a licensed psychologist with a doctorate in clinical psychology from Rutgers University. She has over 30 years' experience working clinically with violent offenders and their victims. She is the owner of Valliere & Counseling Associates, Inc., an outpatient treatment center for interpersonal violence, treating victims and offenders and providing consultation, training, and expert witness services. She serves on the Pennsylvania Sexual Offender Assessment Board, reappointed continuously since 1997. She has published and presented on the topic of sexual assault at international and national conferences. She is recognized as an expert on victim behavior and offenders, testifying nationally and internationally. She has testified before the U.S. Congress and Judiciary Committee regarding sexual assault in the military and consulted with the Department of Defense and the U.S. Department of Justice. She has been interviewed for popular magazines on sexual assault and domestic violence. She has appeared on television and radio shows. Dr. Valliere is the author of *Understanding Victim Response to Interpersonal Violence: A Guide for Investigators and Prosecutors* and *Unmasking the Sexual Offender* published by Routledge.

Successful Prosecution of Intimate Violence

Making it Offender-Focused

Bridget H. Ryan

Veronique N. Valliere

Routledge
Taylor & Francis Group

NEW YORK AND LONDON

Designed cover image: © Getty Images

First published 2024
by Routledge
605 Third Avenue, New York, NY 10158

and by Routledge
4 Park Square, Milton Park, Abingdon, Oxon, OX14 4RN

Routledge is an imprint of the Taylor & Francis Group, an informa business

ISBN: 978-0-367-64029-3 (hbk)
ISBN: 978-0-367-63445-2 (pbk)
ISBN: 978-1-003-12185-5 (ebk)

DOI: 10.4324/9781003121855

Typeset in Bembo Std
by KnowledgeWorks Global Ltd.

To the victims who taught us what they live through and who they are. To the fellow warriors striving to make the changes necessary for accountability and peace. To the people who taught us and to those who will come after us to ensure that there is always someone standing up for victims at every step of their process.

Contents

Acknowledgments

This book has been a long time in the making and would never be a reality without so many people. First and foremost, my fiancé Rex not only supported me throughout long days, nights, and weekends to find the right voice but also for being a phenomenal copyrighter.

I also want to thank the big brains that I surround myself with daily who were willing to share their knowledge and insight into some very complicated topics and concepts. I would like to specifically acknowledge Dr. Jenifer Markowitz, Judge Doug Miles, and MAJ Vanessa Strobbe.

Last, but certainly not least, I want to acknowledge the two people who took me under their wing and guided me through what became the most rewarding career choice I could have made, the late Ms. Teresa Scalzo and the indomitable Ms. Pam Paziotopolous. Pam was my mentor in the Cook County State's Attorney's Office in the 1990s and gave me my first opportunity to litigate intimate violence cases. She has been my mentor ever since and I owe her for the knowledge and career I have been able to build. She introduced me to Teresa in the early 2000s because she recognized, as I quickly did as well, that Teresa was one of the most knowledgeable, passionate, and vociferous advocates in the fight against intimate violence crime. Sadly, we lost her in 2016, but even today, she remains my best friend and a constant source of inspiration.

Bridget H. Ryan, J.D.

I have had the privilege and honor to be embraced by my legal mentors, who have had the patience and passion to teach me about their system and the openness, trust, and creativity to take in the psychological issues and concerns I had to offer. Through this partnership, I have learned a tremendous amount that allowed me to contribute to this book. I would like to acknowledge the changes that these attorneys have worked so ardently for and who have made the system a bit more hospitable to victims, as well as who have fought for accountability for the offenders.

Luckily, I had the opportunity to co-author this book with someone I learned a great deal from, but I would like to thank Hon. Douglas Miles, Dr. Jen Markowitz, Meghan Tokash, J.D., Hon. Sam Conrad, and so many others who have taken time to work with me, teach me, and formed an often formidable team with me in many of the cases we have tried together. I would also like to acknowledge all the up-and-coming prosecutors, some of whom I had the pleasure of training, which challenge me and bring hope for justice for victims in the future.

Veronique N. Valliere, Psy.D.

Introduction

"Why? Why? Why is this thing about me," the victim demanded, "I didn't do anything! I'm the one that got raped! Doesn't he have to answer for anything? What does it matter?" The woman sat before us, a former prosecutor now a trial expert and a forensic psychologist hired for the case. She was betrayed and livid, justifiably so. The trial counsel had unartfully confronted her on an allegation by her former boyfriend that she was on "psych meds for her mental problems" and had lied to the trial team about the assault. There was, and is, no good answer to her questions. Because in crimes of intimate violence, almost without fail, the victim is the focus, targeted and dissected.

Between us, these authors have been involved in hundreds, if not thousands, of cases of intimate violence, either as a trial attorney, trial consultant, or expert witness. We have had the privilege of working together on dozens. Both of us have dedicated our careers to dealing with cases of intimate violence – the most difficult, complex, heartbreaking, meaningful, and rewarding cases there are. Our experiences have motivated us to write this book, which we hope will be a practical guide to allow you to make a paradigm shift about how best to approach these cases and motivate you to become focused on the perpetrators of such devasting crimes.

Crimes of intimate violence are so difficult partly because our legal system was not designed to address crimes so steeped in confounding human behavior. Who and how does someone commit such a profoundly destructive crime as rape? What on earth can expose and explain the formidable impact of repeated battering on a person? How do we understand a person who loves someone who nearly killed her? Most importantly, what can we learn to shift our perspective on people who have suffered abuse from one of judgment and blame to one of respect and empathy and onto the perpetrator who exploited and weaponized our humanity? These questions have haunted us in trial.

In the last days of writing this book together, these authors provided training on prosecuting sexual assault cases. We had the 35 participants (all trial attorneys) introduce themselves and share what they wanted to get out of the course. Without fail, when the participant mentioned the parties to the case, it was always the victim. "I want to know why the victim makes such terrible choices," said one. "I want to know how to go forward with such bad facts because of the victims in my cases," said another. Over and over again, we heard comments about victims, bad facts, and how to even pursue sexual assault and rape cases. Not once did someone say that they wanted to understand, expose, or explain the perpetrator to their factfinders. The reiteration of these experiences over two decades finally put the fire in these two tired warriors to write this book.

Throughout this book, we will address the societal myths and biases that facilitate intimate violence and hinder our ability to prosecute it reliably. We will try to imbue you with our passion

DOI: 10.4324/9781003121855-1

and motivation to turn the focus onto the offender, taking that glaring spotlight off the victim. We strive to give you practical skills and attainable means to become offender-focused. Most of all, we want to encourage more prosecutors to become fellow soldiers in our battle against intimate violence.

Intimate violence is a blight on our society. It is a public health problem. It is lethal. Intimate violence has far-reaching costs to our communities socially, psychologically, and financially. Intimate violence offenders are dangerous to their victims, their children, their pets, law enforcement, and innocent bystanders. Intimate violence offenders, including those who commit sexual assault, domestic violence, and child and elder abuse, are successful and go without consequences. Intimate violence is under-reported, in part because the offenders abuse people who love them. In this book, we will ask you to help change that, offering tools to empower you to prosecute these crimes more effectively. The first step is becoming offender-focused in your thinking and skills.

By the time the victim comes forward, having made a report to authorities, the victim has the Herculean task of deciding to tell. The victim's decision to report is the pivotal point in every case of intimate violence, the inception of the prosecution. Because of this, it is worth remembering that before a victim reported, that victim had to become offender-focused. The victim had to decide to sacrifice privacy and control, face loss and grief, and become entirely vulnerable to the process and the offender in order to report. In reporting, the victim risked judgment, blame, disbelief, rejection, and retaliation. That victim went through a process to determine that it was the offender who should be exposed and held accountable, only to become involved in a system that would scrutinize her. By becoming offender-focused in your investigation and prosecution of intimate violence, you will at least meet the victims where they have struggled to be.

Throughout this book, we will refer mostly to men as the offenders and women as the victims. This is not only reflective of our experience but also reflective of statistics and crime rates that demonstrate that most offenders of intimate violence are men and most victims are women. However, be clear, men can be victims, and women can be offenders. Children, the disabled, the elderly, and the mentally ill are populations that are raped and abused at a significant rate due to their vulnerability. Many populations of victims will present challenges to your cases or be unable or unwilling to cooperate. Using the premise of offender-focused prosecution, this book should help arm you to go forward confidently, knowing that the victim is not the issue; the offender is. The cases and examples we refer to are cases from our experiences.

This book offers general legal strategies and advice. It is the readers' responsibility to understand the law and procedures of their own jurisdiction and use the provided information appropriately in their legal framework.

Our ultimate aspiration in this book is to help you do what is likely your desire – to contribute to a safer world, to bring accountability and justice to someone who is harmful. Because you are reading this book, we know that this is true.

Building a Better Foundation

A Better You

Chapter 1

Myths and Misinformation
Barriers to Believing

"Don't forget, nothing was ever reported. None of them ever reported it," the defense attorney asserted in his closing argument, defending a man convicted of the sexual abuse of nine boys. "I mean, she texted him! She sat on his lap! Who does that after they are raped," the attorney questioned the jury in closing. Another defendant had his minister come to the stand to testify about his character and behavior with his grandchildren. "She loved him, she wasn't scared of him at all," the minister told the jury, describing the congregant as a "loving, kind, peaceful grandfather." "He loved teaching, he was dedicated to it," the accused father argued, "Why would he jeopardize that, tell me? Why?" A victim of intimate partner violence laments, "I know I just stayed. But it's not like he hit me all the time, hardly ever. He just had a bad temper, mostly when he drank."

Intimate violence is devastating. But it may not be as devastating to a victim as being dismissed, disbelieved, or subject to the misinformation and biases of others, especially those involved in the investigation and prosecution of interpersonal violence. Each person in the vignettes above relied on myths, misinformation about victims, and fallacies about violent offenders. As a prosecutor or investigator, not only will you face these biases and the misinformation about intimate violence in your judge, juries, or panels but also will face them in yourself.

Despite reform, education, and awareness, rates of sexual violence have steadily risen in the U.S. through the last decade (Statista, 2021), with an average of over 460,000 people victimized a year (Rape, Abuse, & Incest National Network [RAINN], n.d.). Globally, the rates are also rising, worsening during the COVID pandemic to 45% of women (Emandi et al., 2021; Goody, 2021; World Health Organization, 2021). Additionally, successful prosecution of sexual violence in the U.S. remains low, with less than 1% of reported assaults resulting in felony convictions (RAINN, n.d.; Van Dam, 2018).

Rates of intimate partner violence are also rising, again exacerbated by the pandemic (Piquero et al., 2021). Some research suggests that prosecution of domestic violence is improving in specific ways due to policies regarding mandatory arrests and "no-drop" policies in domestic violence cases. However, these changes do not necessarily reflect a change in attitudes, information, or biases (Del Valle, 2011). Recent statistics show a significant drop in prosecution rates of domestic violence, a problem compounded by the rise in intimate partner violence due to the pandemic and the fact that the court often drops misdemeanor charges in domestic violence cases (AP News, 2019; Barr & Topping, 2020).

How is intimate violence increasing, both sexual and physical, and why are we failing to address it effectively in the criminal justice system? One highly influential factor is our continued acceptance of and reliance on misinformation about violence, guided and filtered by our personal and societal biases.

DOI: 10.4324/9781003121855-3

Biases and Their Impact on Investigation and Prosecution

Biases are predispositions or preferences toward or against something, usually in an unfair way. Merriam-Webster dictionary (n.d.) defines bias as "an inclination of temperament or outlook, especially a personal and sometimes unreasoned judgment, prejudice." Biases are "hidden forces" that impact our perceptions and decision-making, sometimes causing problems in our ability to see the truth or make "logical" decisions (Ariely, 2008). They serve as a cognitive shortcut to organizing information. Numerous biases influence perception and decision-making, impacting how we think about the world in ways that we may not be conscious of and may need to be corrected for, leading to problematic and inaccurate outcomes.

Decades of research show that all of us have biases, they are highly consistent, and they can predict decision-making (Hilbert, 2012). Biases impact the criminal justice process on every level, especially in cases of intimate violence. From the victim and perpetrator to the findings of the jury, judge, or panel, biases can hamper investigations, contribute to faulty interpretations of behavior, and obscure the facts of the case. Effective investigators and prosecutors must understand what biases they carry, how these biases can impact the case, and how to correct them in themselves and others.

While there are many, many types of biases that impact our decision-making, there are a few more salient and influential that impact decision-making for those involved in the criminal justice system. These biases are reflected throughout the process, from the victim's first disclosure to law enforcement through jury deliberations.

Confirmation Bias

Confirmation bias is our tendency to focus on or collect information that supports our pre-existing beliefs. Once a belief is in place and we have invested in it, we collect and interpret information to confirm it (Kahneman, 2011). Consider how influential this bias could be in cases of interpersonal violence. Confirmation bias can protect the offender when the offender's community believes he is "not like that," volunteering to provide character statements asserting the perpetrator's innocence. If investigating officers believe that all victims lie, that 50% of allegations are fabricated, or that sex workers cannot be raped, the case can be mishandled or disposed of from the outset. If the perpetrator has successfully convinced others that his wife is "bipolar" or lying to seek custody, the case can be turned away from the truth of the abuse.

Addressing misinformed beliefs in all players of the prosecutorial process is crucial, given the power and influence of confirmation bias. Confirmation bias influences the victim's reporting, interview questions, collection of evidence, and acceptance or presentation of a case. A juror's confirmation bias may lead to failure to convict. Particularly dangerous is if the players maintain beliefs that blame victims or excuse perpetrators or if they adhere to myth acceptance in cases of sexual assault or intimate violence. If misinformation is not addressed during the presentation of a case, the presence and potency of confirmation bias can determine the outcome despite the evidence presented.

Hindsight Bias

Hindsight bias is how new information affects our recollection and perception of past events. Hindsight bias creates the belief that the outcome of an event is inevitable and that we should have known or seen it coming. It is no more visible than in the revisionist examination of victims' behaviors and choices. Hindsight bias has long been known to increase or even *cause* victim blaming in cases of sexual assault (Janoff-Bulman et al., 1985). Why did she do that? Why didn't she do that? Why did she go home with him, drink more, not see the "red flags," leave?

Hindsight bias also creates other pressures on the victim, especially regarding the victims' memories of or preceding the event. In an assault case, the victim may not have any clear memory of what time it was, how long it lasted, how many drinks were served, what the perpetrator was wearing, or a myriad of other irrelevant details that only become relevant during a trial. Remember, the victim did not know the outcome, so they would not have been trying to memorize the event "in case" it ended up at trial. Instead, the victim was experiencing an event that would not have required special attentiveness at the time it was occurring. Only after the assault occurred is this attention to detail required.

Hindsight bias can impact witnesses to crimes as well. Upon retrospect, witnesses may highlight or reinterpret their memories to fit outcomes. For example, witnesses whose statements are taken close to the event might more accurately report their impressions, while those same witnesses, perhaps those protective of the offender, may now remember that the victim was flirtatious or provocative, thereby "asking for it," at the time of the trial. As we will advocate throughout this book, doing a thorough, offender-focused investigation will help minimize the impact of hindsight bias when the attention is on the offender's actions and corroboration of the victim.

It is critical to remember that in cases of interpersonal violence, the event was *not* inevitable or foreseeable. The victim made decisions based on what the victim understood at the time. The victim did not know that rape would be the outcome of going out for drinks. The wife did not know that the battering was inevitable for speaking to a man at the business function. It is inherent and inevitable that we know the outcome at the time of the investigation and prosecution. We have the luxury of looking backward, knowing that a crime has been committed. It is critical to remember that the victim did not know the outcome and that the offender did know the intended outcome. Addressing the hindsight bias in your case will help you guard against the temptation to defend the victim, focusing instead on the offender's knowledge of his own intentions, decisions, and motivations.

Halo Effect and Attractiveness of Defendants

The halo effect is that bias that influences our perceptions of someone as a whole based on only a limited aspect or experience of that person. It can be positive, like when a good first impression, physical attractiveness, or positive experience with someone gives us the tendency to generalize that to an overall positive belief about someone or their character. Suppose we are responding to the halo effect. In that case, it might contribute to dismissing a report of domestic violence because the perpetrator was a great employee, a good soldier, or goes to Church weekly. It can also be negative, resulting in overall negative attributions to another's character if there have been negative experiences with or performance of that person. Physical attractiveness is associated with the bias that "beautiful equals good" and can contribute to the halo effect. For example, research has shown that attractive defendants were acquitted more often and given lesser sentences (Gunnell & Ceci, 2010); attractive victims are perceived as more credible when reporting intimate partner violence (Hall et al., 2022).

The impact of the halo effect can be seen in many recent high-profile cases, including the case of Larry Nassar, Jerry Sandusky, and Bill Cosby. It is easy to identify how these men benefited from the halo of their status, achievements, or television personality. The halo effect has a detrimental impact on our ability to detect child sexual abuse (Scurich & Dietz, 2021). Perpetrators are acutely aware of this bias, creating and promoting perceptions of themselves as "good," "nice," devoted, or caring individuals (Lanning & Dietz, 2014; Valliere, 2023).

The "devil" effect is the halo effect in reverse. When we think someone is unattractive, when we have had a negative interaction with someone, or after we have formed a negative impression, we tend to attribute negative traits to that person. Imagine then the power of the halo effect in a case of domestic violence. Often the perpetrator is calm, reasonable, and presents well in public. Contrast this with a traumatized, angry, and distressed victim. The police show up for a call. The perpetrator is calm and attempts to explain his overwrought wife, who screams for the police to leave (because she is terrified). Or consider the victim who storms into the bar to scream at her husband for leaving her without diapers for the baby he promised to bring home. The witnesses to this event could get an inaccurately negative impression of the victim, even though the offender created the hostile situation. Victims can be uncooperative, erratic, hostile, and frightened – difficult for law enforcement and prosecutors to work with throughout the case. The offender not only uses the halo effect to bolster his support but also discredits and negatively describes the victim to others, possibly confirmed by the listener's own experiences with the victim.

Ideal Victim Construct

The ideal victim is an archetype for victims who are blameless for their victimization and who act as expected during and after their victimization (Randall, 2011). A "good" victim is not a victim who "brought it on" herself by risk-taking, drinking, "poking the bear," or making "bad choices." An ideal victim does not include a sex worker, an unfaithful spouse, an addicted person, or someone with mental health issues. Research shows that we still subscribe to the ideal victim construct where a "legitimate" victim who is the ideal victim gets more sympathy and credibility than an "illegitimate" victim (Lewis et al., 2019). The media portrays women victims in juxtapose to "innocent" or "ideal" child victims and women as victims who deserve to be blamed, using graphic violence against the victims in a desensitizing, marginalizing way because women are not "pure" (DiBennardo, 2018). Because we continue to blame victims, offenders seek victims with vulnerabilities, choosing or creating victims who are not ideal, understanding and exploiting this bias. This category includes male victims.

Binary Bias

Binary bias or binary thinking is "all-or-nothing" thinking, the tendency to seek clarity by simplifying a continuum into two categories (Grant, 2021). "Good or bad" and "innocent or guilty" are examples of these dichotomies. Binary bias is dangerous in complex cases of intimate violence. It compels investigators and prosecutors to deny, avoid, or try to hide challenges, "bad facts," or otherwise defined "problems" in the case to produce an ideal victim and a monstrous perpetrator. Victims themselves will hide facts that make them look less ideal or exaggerate other elements to support the fear they were genuinely feeling. Some examples include the victim who denies prior sexual contact with the perpetrator, asserts that she never cursed at or slapped the batterer, or swears she was not cheating on her husband who raped her.

You will sometimes encounter serious complications in your cases. The perpetrator might appear to be a likable guy who comes off as a doofus, seeming like he could have easily "mistaken" flirting for consent, instead of being a "predator." The victim might be hostile, angry, and retaliatory, especially if she has undergone years of abuse. If law enforcement, investigators, or prosecutors are prone to binary thinking, the cases could be dismissed immediately when they determine your case is not a "good" case. Even in the most presumably "objective" roles, binary thinking can dictate the course of the case. One study showed that even crime lab personnel asked police only to submit DNA samples from "real" rape cases for testing (Campbell & Fehler-Cabral, 2020)! "Real" rapes versus "not real" rapes is a type of binary thinking established and reinforced by rape myths and rape myth acceptance (RMA), as described below.

Ignoring the Base Rate: The Base-Rate Fallacy

When we ignore the base rate, we mistakenly focus on individual factors or features of a particular situation to contradict the likelihood that the base rate is true. We ignore information about the rate of occurrence, not giving it proper weight (American Psychological Association, n.d.). This phenomenon makes people consistently assert that victims lie about being raped or abused. When we have trained law enforcement or prosecutors, there is a constant discussion of false allegations that comprise "50% of the allegations" that the attendees have seen. Other examples of intimate violence include that women "cry rape," that it is "easy" to get a false conviction or false confession, or that men are not victims of sexual assault.

All these issues are contradicted by facts that are ignored by society and the criminal justice system. Attending to the base rate of false or fabricated allegations would lead to believing allegations from the onset, not approaching them with skepticism and disbelief. Epstein and Goodman (2019) use the term institutionalized skepticism to describe the pervasive pattern of discounting and dismissing victims of intimate partner violence. Research has repeatedly debunked the belief that there is a high rate of false allegations of sexual assault. When the research is rigorous and informed, the rate of false allegations is consistently between 2% and 10% of the studied allegations (Lisak et al., 2010). Despite this, the public, especially men, and law enforcement, remain certain that victims are fabricating reports of assault at a very high rate (Huntington et al., 2020; McMillan, 2018). False or fabricated allegations of sexual assault rates are similar to fabricated allegations of other crimes. Nevertheless, the media pays significant attention to any allegation deemed "false," even if it is merely unprovable. Allegations, like the one against Justice Kavanagh, were not proven *fabricated*; they just could not be proven.

Sexual assault and intimate violence are far under-reported. That is a base-rate fact. It goes undetected by even those closest to victims. These are private, secret crimes, generally without witnesses. But so are other crimes, another fact ignored. Arsonists do not light buildings on fire in front of the police! It is well known that intimate violence crimes are difficult to prosecute, with only a small fraction reaching the courtroom. It is not easy for victims to "cry rape." The #MeToo movement was supposed to illuminate the prevalence of sexual assault in society – instead, the backlash has increased skepticism of victim disclosure (de Roos & Jones, 2020).

Knowing and attending to the base rate of intimate crimes is imperative. Believing is not biased; it is logical based on the known prevalence of these crimes and the low prevalence of false allegations. Not only are fabricated allegations rare but they are also easily detected, have similar features, and rarely make it through the criminal justice system (De Zutter, 2021; Newman, 2018). Allegations that are messy with confounding elements like consensual acts, reports of intimacy, and victim cooperation with the offender are more likely to be dismissed; yet, these messy facts are the elements associated with true allegations (De Zutter, 2021)!

This is not a comprehensive list of the relevant biases that impact cases of intimate violence. Victims and perpetrators are impacted by racial and cultural biases in the system. LGBTQ+ individuals face biases that impact help-seeking, disclosure, and involvement in the criminal justice process. There are biases that prevent us from believing that people "like us" could commit violence. And there is a bias toward denying that terrible things happen or toward believing that the world is fair and manageable and that we can control the risks we face. Unfortunately, sexual assault and intimate partner violence are issues that violate all the norms and expectations we hope to maintain in our world.

Commonly Held Myths and Misconceptions about Intimate Violence

From the moment of the crime, biases, acceptance of myths, and misinformation regarding intimate violence or sexual assault significantly impact your case. The victim who believes she "asked for it" will not call for help. The offender who believes he "didn't really rape her" because he did not use physical violence will be supported in his assertion by his friends and jurors. The officer who believes real rape involves a stranger or that intimate partner violence is a "domestic dispute" will fail to investigate or make an arrest. Jurors who adhere to the belief of the "monster" offender and "ideal" victim will be confounded by the victim cheating on her husband – what red-blooded man wouldn't be angry?

Intimate violence often lacks the "hard" evidence investigators, prosecutors, and juries seek. Medical evidence is typically unavailable, especially in delayed disclosures. Much of the evidence is victim testimony. Given this, it is expected that the players in the prosecutorial process will rely on extra-legal factors to guide decision-making, including myths, biases, and misinformation (Cossins, 2020). These extra-legal factors include character evidence against the victim, RMA, the relationship between the perpetrator and victim, and lack of physical injury. Decades of research have proven that jurors will turn to their own beliefs and expectations about how sexual assault and partner violence should look, resulting in low rates of prosecution of offenders (Cossins, 2020).

This systemic dismissal or skepticism extends to extremely serious and potentially deadly events, like cases that include non-fatal strangulation. Strangulation is an extremely serious act associated with dramatically increased lethality for victims. Despite this, non-fatal strangulation is approached with skepticism during prosecution (Epstein & Goodman, 2019). According to research, there is a systemic failure to understand the neurological impact of trauma and strangulation, inaccurate interpretations of victims' courtroom behavior, and negative stereotypes of victims' motivations for reporting and help-seeking (Epstein & Goodman, 2019). The "reflexive dismissal" of reports of domestic assault creates more barriers to reporting and prosecution and replicates the betrayal and psychological abuse that the victim has already experienced from the perpetrator. The system has little understanding of non-fatal strangulation, a common weapon perpetrators use. Reliance on physical evidence (typically lacking) instead of the victims' reports leads to failures in prosecution, reiterating the need for education of law enforcement in thorough investigations of abuse (Reckdenwald et al., 2020).

Acceptance of Rape Myths

Rape myths are a complex set of false beliefs and values maintained and perpetuated in our society (Lonsway & Fitzgerald, 1994). These myths profoundly impact how society perceives and reacts to sexual violence. Rape myths excuse sexual violence, shift the responsibility of sexual violence from the perpetrator, and blame the victim for being assaulted. Rape myths include the idea that women lie about being assaulted, that a drunk victim is partly responsible for what happens, that resistance is necessary to label something a rape, and that victims "ask for it" if they act or dress a certain way. When someone accepts these myths, they endorse ideas that blame the victim and mitigate the culpability and intent of the perpetrator. If a sexual assault does not comport to the internalized idea of "real rape," it is not taken seriously. A survey example of these myths is the Acceptance of Modern Myths about Sexual Aggression (Gerger et al., 2013).

RMA and its influence have been studied for decades. Despite all the education available, they persist. Not only do they persist but also they are held more tightly and overtly by men (See, 2017). They influence law enforcement attitudes and actions (Constantinou, 2021; Garza & Franklin, 2020). They affect jury perceptions and decisions. The impact of these myths is always in favor of the perpetrator and against the victims. Jurors who uphold these myths are more likely to find a perpetrator not guilty of a sexual crime (Booth et al., 2018). Men who adhere to rape myths are more likely to commit sexual violence (Yapp & Quayle, 2018). Rape myths are so powerful that they even impact crime lab personnel's decision-making when they request that police only submit evidence on "real" sexual assaults (Campbell & Fehler-Cabral, 2020), defined as violent stranger assaults. The crime lab cautioned that "shady" cases were not worth testing. The cases included offenders known by the victims and sexual assault of adolescents and sex workers.

Offenders use rape myths to deny, minimize, manipulate, and get away with the offense. Victims who adhere to rape myths fail to acknowledge or identify themselves as victims of assault, even when they have experienced chargeable crimes. Rape myths are alive and well, impacting our cases. A conviction was far more likely when a rape included a stranger perpetrator, an outdoor assault, and some level of violence, including verbal violence (Lundrigan et al., 2019). This type of rape is unusual. It is well known that most victims are assaulted by someone they know.

The Relationship Factor

One element of rape myths is that the actor is a stranger. Stranger perpetrators in intimate types of crimes are taken more seriously. When a rape reflects the myth, conviction is more likely. Specifically, a perpetrator is more likely to be convicted if he committed the offense against a stranger outdoors, using some type of violence, and penetrating the victim (Lundrigan et al., 2019). Those of us who have worked in these cases for a while understand how unusual this scenario is in real life! In most cases of intimate violence, physical and sexual, the victim and perpetrator are in a relationship.

Having a relationship with a perpetrator is very detrimental to a victim. The perpetrator uses the relationship as a weapon, a way to have access to the victim and a means to abuse the victim. The relationship itself is damaging to the victim, who experiences all the complicated feelings of love, protection, betrayal, fear, and grief involving the abuser. The offender uses the relationship against the victim, confronting the victim with her promises to love and honor him or activating her guilt and shame because she is "sending him to jail." The relationship obscures the offender's motivations while providing a reason for the victim's motive to lie – retaliation, jealousy, vengeance. It is difficult for an offender to claim that the stranger victim is lying because she wants the house, the kids, or to get back at him for cheating!

The criminal justice system protects the offender who has a relationship with the victim. The non-stranger offender benefits throughout the entire course of the process. When there is a relationship between the offender and victim, law enforcement and juries think that violence or sexual assault is "different" from "real" sexual assault or violence, the relationship mitigating the assessment of the offender's intent or culpability (Hine & Murphy, 2018). Even nurses blame the victim when she has a relationship with the perpetrator (Persson et al., 2018). The idea of prior consent can confound the identification of sexual assault, not only for investigators and juries but also for the victims themselves. Relationships with perpetrators lead to the victims' continued contact with the offender, something people find hard to understand or counterintuitive. Even with child victims, juries were more likely to acquit an offender if the child had continued contact with the person (Stolzenberg & Lyon, 2014)! As if children can choose to stop a relationship with an abusive adult! A relationship between the perpetrator and victim is a powerful determinant in cases of intimate violence. A relationship not only impacts findings of guilt as a whole but also impacts a jury's assessment of the seriousness of charges. Juries are reluctant to find an offender guilty of first-degree rape, as opposed to lesser charges, in intimate partner rape (Lynch et al., 2019).

Victim Blaming

When we blame a victim for the perpetrator's behavior, the cases become very difficult. Throughout this book, we will highlight how victims get blamed. They blame themselves. The perpetrators blame them. Society blames them. Victim blaming comes in overt and subtle, insidious ways. Victims are blamed if they were drinking, provocative, sexy, in the wrong place, and on and on. In a culture of victim blaming, it is easier to blame someone for being vulnerable to a crime than to see the perpetrators' true nature. The victim "asked for it" in some way – drinking, dressing a certain way, acting sexually, or being alone. The victim made "bad" choices that made her vulnerable, which a predatory person expectedly exploits. "What did she think was going to happen," we ask. "She poked the bear," a prosecutor asserted, explaining why he could not hold a football player responsible for cold-cocking his wife, captured on camera.

People try to soften the blaming with professed empathy, saying things like, "Not that she deserved it, but …" followed by comments about the victim's drinking, friends, and choices. Some researchers termed this thinking "benevolent rape myth acceptance" (Davies et al., 2012). We see the same dynamic in "prevention" programs that suggest women drink less, have a "buddy" wherever they go, or try not to attract attention. There is the idea that the victim should "know better" and assumes the risk of being raped if she makes certain choices. Victims in relationships with abusers face the same blame. She should leave, be more assertive, kick him out, and stop "allowing" her partner to abuse her. On the surface, these statements seem to hold the perpetrator responsible for the abuse, but there is underlying blame for the victim's "failure" to stop it.

Alcohol Use by Victim or Perpetrator

When a victim has used alcohol at the time of the offense, the responding officers' likelihood of responding "vigorously" is lessened. Officers are less likely to call in a detective or arrest the suspect (Venema, 2016). Victims are blamed more for being assaulted when drinking (Grubb & Turner, 2012). Perhaps most significantly, victims blame themselves more and experience more shame when they have been drinking when assaulted (Kahn et al., 2003). Shame and self-blame are significant barriers to reporting. In cases of incapacitated rape, when the victim is very intoxicated or unconscious, the victim faces being blamed more when reporting, mainly because the offender has not had to use force or the victim did not resist (Brown et al., 2018). The offender rapes a victim who is entirely incapable of self-defense, then benefits because no force was necessary and she could not resist! Alcohol use benefits the offenders throughout the case.

Bias, Myth Acceptance, and Misinformation: The Impact on the Criminal Justice System

Beyond the fact that myths and misinformation continue to create societal hurdles for understanding victims and holding offenders accountable, they significantly impact the judicial process for victims and prosecutors of intimate violence. Judges rely on biases to determine what are "real" cases of domestic violence versus "frivolous" cases (Kafka et al., 2019). Prosecutors do not take complicated cases to trial for fear that there will be an acquittal or because the victim is challenging or uncooperative. Law enforcement and juries appeared to be the most well-studied groups regarding how bias and myth acceptance affect the cases. As critical players in the prosecutorial process, the implications of this research are important to understand.

The Impact on Law Enforcement and Investigation

The case attrition rate of sexual assault and intimate violence cases is a serious issue. The attrition begins with responding officers. First responding police officers significantly impact whether a victim cooperates, what evidence is collected, and whether a case moves forward. Responding police officers must make numerous decisions and judgments at the onset of a case. Officers can make poor, incomplete, and inaccurate judgments if these decisions, perceptions, or conclusions are based on biases or myths.

Studies show that police officers are still making judgments on what they perceive as a "good" case. RMA in officers is related to less vigorous response to assault allegations, especially if the victim was drinking, resulting in fewer arrests and detective involvement, driven by whom the officer blames (Venema, 2016). In a meta-analysis of studies on police decision-making, several factors were identified as significantly impacting officer decision-making in sexual assault cases (Lapsey et al., 2022). Victim cooperation and available witnesses increased the likelihood of a proactive response by officers. However, the assessment of subject blameworthiness was significant as well. An assessment of blameworthiness was mitigated by rape myths, increasing police assessments of perpetrator blame when the victim overtly resisted and had injury, or when the perpetrator used a weapon. In other words, when the rape met the myth.

Not only can law enforcement make poor decisions based on myth acceptance but they can also contribute to secondary trauma and make it far less likely that a victim will continue to cooperate with the case. Over one-third of sexual assault victims in one study did not pursue cooperation after the initial interview (Murphy et al., 2014). Black women who have been sexually assaulted identify apprehension about law enforcement and a negative response to their initial disclosure of assault as significant barriers to reporting (Tillman et al., 2010). However, law enforcement who provide a more favorable initial experience to victims through support, without blaming the victim or being otherwise negative to the victim, have a significant positive effect resulting in more cooperation with prosecution (Patterson, 2011). Other good news includes findings that women might be starting to believe that "things have changed" in law enforcement regarding reporting abuse even after they experienced disbelief, skepticism, and a poor understanding of the impact of trauma by law enforcement (Johnson, 2017). The fact that victims continue to experience these issues speaks to the need for further training and education of law enforcement rather than simple fixes like having more women officers. Given that both men and women endorse myths and victim blaming, it is education, not the gender of the officer, that will make a difference.

The Impact on Jury Decision-Making

Research shows robust support for the conclusion that even now, jurors continue to endorse and make decisions regarding sexual assault cases based on myth acceptance and problematic beliefs or biases about victim behavior (Leverick, 2020). Jurors rely on extra-legal information when confronted with decision-making in cases of sexual assault where there is no "hard" evidence (Cossins, 2020). Jurors continue to rely on misinformation that blames the victim, overestimates false allegations, excuses the accused, and mischaracterizes "real" rape (Leverick, 2020). In her analysis of both qualitative and quantitative studies, Leverick found "overwhelming" evidence that jurors rely on "false and prejudicial" beliefs about rape and rape victims. She concluded that there is support for the idea that juror education can change the effect of these biases (Leverick, 2020).

Jury bias impacts cases of intimate violence in many ways. In sexual assault cases, jurors expected victims to fight back and suffer injury. Jurors are more likely to see a marital or intimate relationship as a mitigating factor in rape, resulting in convictions of lesser charges (Lynch et al., 2019). Jurors are impacted by myth-related issues like injury, the presence of a weapon, victims' emotionality during testimony, and the presence of medical evidence (Cossins, 2020). As discussed, juries are prone to blame victims and exonerate perpetrators. Luckily, juror education about biases, myths, and the realities of intimate violence proves useful in combating misinformation's influence on juror decision-making and outcome (Ellison & Munro, 2013).

Summary

Bias and myth acceptance are serious social issues contributing to the continued rise of intimate violence. In a society where victims are met with blaming and skepticism and offenders are not held accountable for their actions, it is only reasonable to assume that the rates of violence will escalate. As an actor in the criminal justice system, it is your responsibility to identify and address these biases – in yourself and your case – in order to best ensure justice. Successful efforts in investigating and prosecuting cases of intimate violence, especially by keeping the case offender-focused, will reinforce for victims that things "are changing." In conclusion:

- Biases and misinformation about intimate violence continue to be a serious problem, negatively impacting victims and the successful prosecution of these cases.
- Numerous biases affect how a report of intimate violence is judged and managed from the moment of the crime – from the victim through the prosecutorial process.
- Misinformation and myth acceptance can be addressed effectively by education prior to and during the presentation of the case.
- An offender-focused case puts the spotlight where it should be, on the offender, minimizing the reinforcement of victim blaming while magnifying the intentions and actions of the offender.

References

American Psychological Association. (n.d.). Base rate fallacy. In *APA Dictionary of Psychology*. https://dictionary.apa.org/base-rate-fallacy

AP News. (2019, December 4). Court often drops charges in misdemeanor domestic violence. *AP News*. https://apnews.com/article/05594479df0cef29224d014fe258df1f

Ariely, D. (2008). *Predictably irrational: The hidden forces that shape our decisions*. Harper Collins, Inc.

Barr, C., & Topping, A. (2020, April 30). Domestic abuse prosecutions fell by 24% at the end of 2019. *The Guardian*. https://www.theguardian.com/society/2020/apr/30/domestic-abuse-prosecutions-fell-by-25-at-end-of-2019

Booth, N., Willmott, D., & Boduszek, D. (2018). Rape myths and misconceptions. *The Law Society Gazette*. https://www.lawgazette.co.uk/commentary-and-opinion/rape-myths-and-misconceptions/5068719. article

Brown, A., Horton, J., & Guillory, A. (2018). The impact of victim alcohol consumption and perpetrator use of force on perceptions in an acquaintance rape vignette. *Violence and Victims, 33(1)*, 40–52. https://dx.doi.org/10.1891/0886-6708.VV-D-16-00099

Campbell, R., & Fehler-Cabral, G. (2020). "Just bring us the real ones:" The role of forensic crime laboratories in guarding the gateway to justice for sexual assault victims. *Journal of Interpersonal Violence*. https://doi.org/10.1177/0886260520951303

Constantinou, A. (2021). *Applied research on policing for police*. Springer. https://doi.org/10.1007/978-3-030-76377-0_7

Cossins, A. (2020). *Closing the justice gap for adult and child sexual assault*. Palgrave McMillan.

Davies, M., Gilston, J., & Rogers, P. (2012). Examining the relationships between male rape myth acceptance, female rape myth acceptance, victim blame, homophobia, gender roles, and ambivalent sexism. *Journal of Interpersonal Violence, 27(14)*, 2807–2823. https://doi.org/10.1177/0886260512438281

de Roos, M., & Jones, D. (2020). Self-affirmation and false allegations: The effects on responses to disclosures of sexual victimization. *Journal of Interpersonal Violence*, 1–24. https://doi.org/10.1177/0886260520980387

De Zutter, A. (2021). True and false allegations of rape. In N. Deslauriers-Varin & C. Bennell (Eds.), *Criminal investigations of sexual offenses: Techniques and challenges*. Springer.

Del Valle, S. (2011). *Biases in domestic violence criminal decision making: Are system actors lenient in domestic violence cases?* Cornell Law School Inter-University Graduate Student Conference Papers. http://scholarship.law.cornell.edu/lps_clacp/51

DiBennardo, R. (2018). Ideal victims and monstrous offenders: How the news media represent sexual predators. *Socius*. https://doi.org/10.1177/2378023118802512

Ellison, L., & Munro, V. (2013). Better the devil you know? 'Real rape' stereotypes and the relevance of a previous relationship in (mock) juror deliberations. *The International Journal of Evidence & Proof, 17*, 299–322. https://doi.org/10.1350/ijep.2013.17.4.433

Emandi, R., Encarnacion, J., Seck, P., & Tabaco, R. (2021). *Measuring the shadow pandemic: Violence against women during COVID-19*. UNWomen. https://data.unwomen.org/sites/default/files/documents/Publications/Measuring-shadow-pandemic.pdf

Epstein, D., & Goodman, L. (2019). *Doubting domestic violence survivors' credibility and dismissing their experiences*, 167 U. Pa. L. Rev. 399. https://scholarship.law.upenn.edu/penn_law_review/vol167/iss2/3

Garza, A., & Franklin, C. (2020). The effector of rape myth endorsement on police response to sexual assault survivors. *Violence Against Women, 27(3–4)*. https://doi.org/10.1177/1077801220911460

Gerger, H., Kley, H., Bohner, G., & Siebler, F. (2013). *Acceptance of Modern Myths About Sexual Aggression (AMMSA) scale*. Measurement Instrument Database for the Social Science. www.midss.ie

Goody, M. (2021, March 9). Nearly 1 in 3 women experience violence: Landmark report from WHO. *NPR*. https://www.npr.org/sections/goatsandsoda/2021/03/09/975358112/nearly-1-in-3-women-experience-violence-landmark-report-from-who

Grant, A. (2021). *Think again: The power of knowing what you don't know*. Viking.

Grubb, A., & Turner, E. (2012). Attribution of blame in rape cases: A review of the impact of rape myth acceptance, gender role conformity and substance use on victim blaming. *Aggression and Violent Behavior, 17(5)*, 443–452.

Gunnell, J., & Ceci, S. (2010). When emotionality trumps reason: A study of individual processing style and juror bias. *Behavioral Sciences and the Law, 28*, 850–877. https://onlinelibrary.wiley.com/doi/pdfdirect/10.1002/bsl.939

Hall, M., Debowska, A., & Hales, G. (2022). The effect of victim attractiveness and type of abuse suffered on attributions of victim blame and credibility in intimate partner violence: A vignette-based online experiment. *Violence Against Women*. https://eprints.whiterose.ac.uk/187504/

Hilbert, M. (2012). Toward a synthesis of cognitive biases: How noisy information processing can bias human decision making. *Psychological Bulletin, 138*(2), 211–237. https://doi.org/10.1037/a0025940

Hine, B., & Murphy, A. (2018). The influence of 'high' vs. 'low' rape myth acceptance on police officers' judgements of victim and perpetrator responsibility, and rape authenticity. *Journal of Criminal Justice.* https://doi.org/10.1016/j.jcrimjus.2018.08.001

Huntington, C., Berkowitz, A., & Orchowski, L. (2020). *False accusations of sexual assault: Prevalence, misperceptions, and implications for prevention work with men and boys.* https://www.researchgate.net/publication/343240574_False_Accusations_of_Sexual_Assault_Prevalence_Misperceptions_and_Implications_for_Prevention_Work_with_Men_and_Boys

Janoff-Bulman, R., Timko, C., & Carli, L. L. (1985). Cognitive biases in blaming the victim. *Journal of Experimental Social Psychology, 39*, 1–17.

Johnson, H. (2017). Why doesn't she just report it? Apprehensions and contradictions for women who report sexual violence to police. *Canadian Journal of Women and the Law, 29*(1), 36–59. https://doi.org/10.3138/cjwl.29.1.36

Kafka, J. M., Moracco, K. E., Barrington, C., & Mortazavi, A. L. (2019). Judging domestic violence from the bench: A narrative analysis of judicial anecdotes about domestic violence protective order cases. *Qualitative Health Research, 29*(8), 1132–1144. https://doi.org/10.1177/1049732318821691

Kahn, A., Jackson, J., Kully, C., Badger, K., & Halvorsen (2003). Calling it rape: Differences in experiences of women who do or do not label their sexual assault as rape. *Psychology of Women Quarterly, 27*, 233–242. https://doi.org/10.1111/1471-6402.00103

Kahneman, D. (2011). *Thinking fast and slow.* Farrar, Straus and Giroux.

Lanning, K. V., & Dietz, P. (2014). Acquaintance molestation and youth-serving organizations. *Journal of Interpersonal Violence, 29*(15), 2815–2838.

Lapsey, D., Campbell, B., & Plumlee, B. (2022). Focal concerns and police decision making in sexual assault cases: A systematic review and meta-analysis. *Trauma, Violence, & Abuse, 23*(4), 1220–1234. https://doi.org/10.1177/1524838021991285

Leverick, F. (2020). What do we know about rape myths and juror decision making? *International Journal of Evidence & Proof, 24*(3), 255–279. https://doi.org/10.1177/1365712720923157

Lewis, J., Hamilton, J., & Elmore, J. (2019). Describing the ideal victim: A linguistic analysis of victim descriptions. *Current Psychology, 40*, 4324–4332. https://doi.org/10.1007/s12144-019-00347-1

Lisak, D., Gardinier, L., Nicksa, S., & Cote, A. (2010). False allegations of sexual assault: An analysis of ten years of reported cases. *Violence Against Woman, 16*(12), 1318–1334. https://doi.org/10.1177/1077801210387747

Lonsway, K. A., & Fitzgerald, L. F. (1994). Rape myths: In review. *Psychology of Women Quarterly, 18*(2), 133–164.

Lundrigan, S., Dhami, M., & Agudelo, K. (2019). Factors predicting conviction in stranger rape cases. *Frontiers in Psychology, 10.* https://doi.org/10.2289/fpsyg.2019.00526

Lynch, K., Golding, J., Jewell, J., Lippert, A., & Wasarhaley, N. (2019). "She is his girlfriend – I believe this is a different situation": Gender differences in perceptions of the legality of intimate partner rape. *Journal of Family Violence, 34*, 213–230. https://doi.org/10.1007/s10896-018-0006-0

McMillan, L. (2018). Police officers' perceptions of false allegations of rape. *Journal of Gender Studies, 27*, 9–21. https://doi.org/10.1080/09589236.2016.1194260

Merriam-Webster. (n.d.) Bias. In *Merriam-Webster.com dictionary.* Retrieved March 11, 2022, from https://www.merriam-webster.com/dictionary/bias

Murphy, S., Edwards, K., Bennett, S., Bibeau, S., & Sichelstiel, J. (2014). Police reporting practices for sexual assault cases in which "the victim does not wish to pursue charges". *Journal of Interpersonal Violence, 29*(1), 144–156. https://doi.org/10.1177/0886260513504648

Newman, S. (2018, September 18). *I've studied false rape claims. The accusation against Kavanaugh doesn't fit the profile.* Vox. https://www.vox.com/first-person/2018/9/18/17874504/kavanaugh-assault-allegation-christine-blasey-ford

Patterson, D. (2011). The linkage between secondary victimization by law enforcement and rape case outcomes. *Journal of Interpersonal Violence, 26*, 328–347. https://doi.org/10.1177/0886260510362889

Persson, S., Dhingra, D., & Grogan, S. (2018). Attributions of victim blame in stranger and acquaintance rape: A quantitative study. *Journal of Clinical Nursing*, 1–10. https://doi.org/10.1111/jocn.14351

Piquero, A., Jennings, W., Jemison, E., Kaukinen, C., & Knaul, F. (2021). Domestic violence during the COVID-19 pandemic – Evidence from a systematic review and meta-analysis. *Journal of Criminal Justice*, *74*. https://doi.org/10.1016/j.jcrimjus.2021.101806

Randall, M. (2011). Sexual assault law, credibility, and "ideal victims": Consent, resistance, and victim blaming. *Canadian Journal of Women and the Law*, *22*. https://doi.org/10.3138/cjwl.22.2.397

Rape, Abuse, & Incest National Network. (n.d.). *Victims of sexual violence: Statistics*. https://www.rainn.org/statistics/victims-sexual-violence

Reckdenwald, A., King, D., & Pritchard, A. (2020). Prosecutorial response to non-fatal strangulation in domestic violence cases. *Violence and Victims*, *35*(2), 160–175. https://doi.org/10.1891/VV-D-18-00105

Scurich, N., & Dietz, P. (2021). Psychological barriers to the detection of child sexual abuse. In D. DeMatteo & K. Scherr (Eds.), *The Oxford handbook of psychology and law*. https://ssrn.com/abstract=3786874

See, W. (2017). *Differences in rape myth acceptance between genders: A systematic review*. PsyArXiv. https://doi.org/10.31234/osf.io/8dns4

Statista. (2021, September 29). *Reported forcible rape rate in the United States from 1990 to 2020*. https://www.statista.com/statistics/191226/reported-forcible-rape-rate-in-the-us-since-1990/

Stolzenberg, S., & Lyon, T. (2014). Evidence summarized in the attorney's closing arguments predicts acquittals in criminal trials of child sexual abuse. *Child Maltreatment*, *19*(2), 119–129. https://doi.org/10.1177/107755951453988

Tillman, S., Bryant-Davis, T., Smith, K., & Marks, A. (2010). Shattering silence: Exploring barriers to disclosure for African-American sexual assault survivors. *Trauma, Violence, & Abuse*, *11*(2), 59–70. https://doi.org/10.1177/1524838010363717

Valliere, V. (2023). *Unmasking the sexual offender*. Routledge Press.

Van Dam, A. (2018, October 6). Less than 1% of rapes lead to felony convictions. At least 89% of victims face emotional and physical consequences. *The Washington Post*. https://www.washingtonpost.com/business/2018/10/06/less-than-percent-rapes-lead-felony-convictions-least-percent-victims-face-emotional-physical-consequences/

Venema, R. (2016). Police officer schema of sexual assault reports: Real rape, ambiguous cases, and false reports. *Journal of Interpersonal Violence*, *31*(5), 872–899. https://doi.org/10.1177/0886260514556765

World Health Organization. (2021, March 9). *Devastatingly pervasive: 1 in 3 women globally experience violence*. World Health Organization. https://www.who.int/news/item/09-03-2021-devastatingly-pervasive-1-in-3-women-globally-experience-violence

Yapp, E., & Quayle, E. (2018). A systematic review of the association between rape myth acceptance and male-on-female sexual violence. *Aggression and Violent Behavior*, *41*. https://doi.org/10.1016/j.avb.2018.05.002

Chapter 2

How Does Anyone Do That?

Understanding the Mind and Motivation
of Offenders

Intimate violence, whether sexual assault or intimate partner violence, is characterized by instrumental violence that serves the offender's needs – emotionally, interpersonally, psychologically, and sexually. Instrumental violence is goal-directed violence, different from reactive or defensive violence, which is a response to a direct threat. The offender has specific objectives for the violence, like sexual gratification, humiliation, oppression, domination, or even stress relief. Patterned violence in a relationship serves the offender in many ways.

For most of us, attaining gratification from hurting another is bewildering. Because it can be so foreign, we rely on misinformation or project our own experiences to explain the behavior or fill in the gaps in our knowledge and experiences. This leads to inaccurate interpretations of behavior as we rely on information that is faulty, superficially makes sense, or is familiar to us. In this chapter, we will explore the misconceptions of offenders who are intimately violent and explore the actual pathways to violence, as well as what tools offenders use to manipulate and influence their victims.

Many complex factors increase the risk of sexual assault or intimate violence or combine to form an offender's beliefs and behaviors. This is not to oversimplify a complicated issue. There are numerous correlates to violence and factors related to increasing the risk of violence. However, in our efforts to acknowledge how multifaceted human behavior is, we can overlook concrete realities that differentiate the abuser or rapist from others who do not abuse. In offender-focused case analysis, it is critical to see past all the excuses or justifications that obscure the offenders' intentions, behaviors, and decisions to commit crimes against others.

Misconceptions about Offenders of Intimate Violence

As society maintains adherence to myths about rape and domestic violence, we continue to hang on to persistent misunderstandings about sexual and domestically violent offenders. Attribution bias impels us to form causal links between an offender's violent and sexual behavior to factors that tend to excuse, overlook, or minimize the offender's character and intention. Offenders continue to be perceived as being reactive, "sick," insecure, or drunk as opposed to skilled actors who are engaging in intentional rewarding behavior with others, able to disregard the impact of their behavior to achieve gratification. Remember, intimate partner violence is a pattern, not an isolated event. Rape, sexual abuse, and sexual harassment are not mistakes or accidents. Below are some of the often-cited *causes* of violence.

"He's Not Like That" – Myth of Identifiability and Typologies

Not only do we crave ideal victims but we also adhere to stereotypes of offenders, stereotypes that are fostered by media – the creepy pedophile, the stranger rapist, the intimate partner offender who is a heterosexual male, and the predator (DiBennardo, 2018; Ramsey, 2015). Picture the

DOI: 10.4324/9781003121855-4

brute in the "wife-beater" being pulled drunk into a police car. This is how we like our offenders to present – easily identifiable. Relying on stereotypes of the "psychopath," the "predator," or the "creep" can blind us to considering that offenders who do not meet our stereotypes could be abusers. This blindness and denial about the insidious normalcy of the intimate violence offender are pervasive, leading to psychological barriers to identifying offense behavior in people we know (Scurich & Dietz, 2021). Though most intimate violence perpetrators are males who abuse females, intimate violence is committed by men against men and women against women, men, and children. Exaggerated portrayals of offenders help them hide.

The "sex maniac" stereotype of offenders of sexual assault can impact your cases. In a number of cases, these authors have been involved in cases where there were acquittals of offenders who *were in the process of sexually assaulting the victim* by their own admissions, but they stopped when the victims' resistance became difficult to override. Two of these cases come to mind. One victim threw up after coming to from being unconscious – the offender had been orally raping her. He stopped to get her water and help her to the bathroom. Another had to put her feet against the offender's chest to push him off and get his fingers out of her vagina. Both men admitted what they were doing; both men stopped. Both were acquitted. "Real" rapists can't stop, according to the myth. The defendants were not monsters.

Reliance on "typologies" of offenders is also hazardous, especially in sexual offenders. Believing that "child molesters" will never have adult victims will blind you to the fact that the perpetrator raped his wife while she slept. Similarly, sexual offenders demonstrate tremendous crossover offenses. Most offenders admit to "crossover" offenses, crossing lines of age, gender, and relationship (Heil et al., 2003; Simons, 2015). Those who abuse adults abuse children. Those who assault males may assault females. When the backlog of untested rape kits was tested, researchers found no consistent MO or victim preferences in the rapes identified as belonging to the same rapist (Lovell et al., 2020). If you believe in the false dichotomy that an offender is either domestically violent or a sex offender, you will not investigate appropriately. In households with domestic or intimate partner violence, child abuse occurs (sexual and physical) up to 50% of the time (Bancroft et al., 2012). Additionally, most victims of battering are victims of sexual assault by the same perpetrator (Bancroft et al., 2012).

Be cognizant of these stereotypes when you are investigating or presenting your case. Do not fall prey to the stereotypes or tell yourself that you would know if the accused is a "real" offender. These offenders are more like us than not, committing their crimes in secrecy while presenting with a prosocial public persona. Often, prosecutors attempt to force a stereotype onto a perpetrator, labeling a college student who rapes an unconscious co-ed as a "predator," magnifying his danger to an implausible level so that the jury rejects the reality. Do not confuse the damage to or impact on the victim with portraying the offender in such an unreal way that the judge or jury thinks you are demonizing instead of prosecuting. When a guy who presents as nice and meek is portrayed as a crazed, drooling rapist, the leap may be too great for the jury to make. Instead, convey how the offender weaponized his normalcy to hide in plain sight.

Alcohol as a Cause of Intimate Violence

Offenders (and the rest of us) desire to blame something else for the offenders' violence or abusive behavior. Drinking serves as a ready excuse for offenders, both sexual and intimate partner offenders. Alcohol use, in the victims or offenders, is correlated with physical and sexual assault for various reasons. But it *does not cause* an offender to commit an offense. Alcohol raises the risk of an offense in those with a propensity for intimate violence and the risk of victimization in intoxicated victims. Alcohol abuse in intimate violence offenders can increase the severity and frequency of abusive or assaultive behaviors (Bancroft et al., 2012).

Alcohol intoxication can decrease inhibitory controls. Inhibitory controls are those external factors that help us manage behavior, like fear of embarrassment or consequences. When we lose sight of these controls, it is a phenomenon called alcohol myopia (Giancola et al., 2010). We get "near-sighted" when drinking, only attending to our strongest urges or states instead of attending to the inhibitory controls, making us more likely to act out on our urges. In offenders who have the urge to be violent or sexually abusive, alcohol use can increase the likelihood of acting out on these urges. In intimate partner violence victims, alcohol use can mute the victim's fear of the offender, impelling the victim to complain, challenge, or confront the abuser about things she has suppressed, escalating the risk of retaliation by the offender.

Alcohol expectancies contribute to accommodating and excusing the abuse for offenders and victims. Alcohol expectancies are beliefs about how alcohol affects our behavior (Davis et al., 2013). When people expect alcohol to cause or facilitate behavior, their beliefs shape behavior when someone is drinking. For example, if someone believes that alcohol makes him more social, he will be more social when he drinks. If a woman believes that alcohol causes her husband's aggression, she will attribute his behavior to the alcohol, not his character. One study showed that intimate violence perpetrators with strong expectations that alcohol makes them violent were over three times more likely to be domestically violent (Field et al., 2004). Assessing and addressing these beliefs is vital if alcohol is involved in an offender-focused case. Voir dire can address the beliefs that the jury may hold, like that someone who is drinking is less responsible for abusive acts. Investigators must confront these beliefs in themselves as well so as not to minimize cases of "marital spats" because one or both of the partners have been drinking.

Finally, alcohol serves the offenders in other ways. For a sexual offender, a victim's alcohol use makes the victim more vulnerable, physically and psychologically. An intoxicated victim's credibility is diminished. An unconscious victim cannot remember. A victim who has been drinking before a sexual assault is more likely to blame herself for the assault, and is more likely to be blamed by others including law enforcement (Grubb & Turner, 2012; Ullman, 2021). Offenders are aware of being able to "blame the booze" and be held less accountable for their crimes.

The Myth of Mental Illness as a Cause for Instrumental Violence

Mental illness is typically considered an acute state of disrupted functioning, perception, and decision-making, sometimes with distorted reality testing, like psychotic disorders or serious mood disorders. Severe anxiety, depression, or schizophrenia are disorders we classify as mental illnesses. More stable and chronic disorders, like personality disorders, are less well understood and typically not considered an acute mental illness. We readily label violent or sexual offenders as "crazy" or "sick" because they engage in behaviors that we cannot understand, like sexually abusing children or battering loved ones. While acute mental illness can be a factor in reactive or defensive violence, acute mental illness is not a potent factor in causing instrumental violence, especially patterned violence like intimate partner violence, ongoing sexual abuse, or premeditated sexual assault. Instrumental violence is goal-directed, can be secretive, and is actively camouflaged by the offender. The relationship between major mental illness and sexual offending and violence is that it makes aggressive people more at risk for further aggression. In and of itself, acute mental illness is not a common cause of violence (DeAngelis, 2021). Most violence is not committed by the seriously mentally ill; most seriously mentally ill people are not violent.

What is correlated highly with violence, especially instrumental violence, are pathological personality traits. When these traits are excessive and disrupt an individual's psychological, interpersonal, and occupational functioning, the traits are diagnosable as a personality disorder.

A personality disorder is defined by the Diagnostic and Statistical Manual – 5th Edition (DSM-5) (American Psychiatric Association, 2013) as an "enduring pattern of inner experience and behavior that deviates markedly from expectations of the person's culture" (p. 645). A personality disorder is *pervasive*, meaning it impacts all spheres of a person's functioning, like thinking, perceiving, and relating. Personality disorders are chronic, inflexible, and stable. The disorder is part of the person's *foundation* – the personality and character.

Personality disorders make up a significant percentage of the mental health diagnoses of violent offenders, including sexual offenders. A correlation between "mental illness" and violence is most often related to a diagnosis of a personality disorder, not another type of acute or severe mental illness. Domestic violence offenders, mass shooters, stalkers, and sexual offenders all demonstrate a significant incidence of personality disorder diagnoses as groups, if they have any diagnosis at all (Bancroft et al., 2012; Eher et al., 2019; Metzi & MacLeish, 2015; Nijdam-Jones et al., 2018; Sorrentino et al., 2018). The personality traits associated with interpersonal violence include entitlement, callousness, grandiosity, exploitiveness, lack of empathy and remorse, and blaming others. These will be discussed further below.

Low Self-Esteem, a Bad Temper, or Adequacy Issues

There is a persistent notion that low self-esteem, anger management problems, trust issues, or feelings of inadequacy are the root causes of intimate violence and sexual offending. Offenders will blame their "low self-esteem" for why they assaulted their victim. Therapists and others will buy this excuse. Some offenders say they are shy or anxious. Some say they are inadequate, "scared" of women, or have "intimacy deficits." The intimate partner offender and the victim will both say he has anger management issues or a "temper" problem. Think through the validity of these assertions. It is essential to differentiate between what *causes* or motivates an offender to offend versus the offender's state when he presents himself to others, especially after being caught and facing the consequences.

These internal states are mediated by the offender's perceptions, expectations, and beliefs. If an offender expects total loyalty and admiration, he might develop "trust" issues or feel inadequate when his partner does not service his ego adequately. An offender with distorted expectations of how he should be treated or obeyed might have "anger issues" when the world does not meet these expectations. Look at the idea that offenders are motivated to offend because they have "low self-esteem." Low self-esteem is characterized by a poor feeling of worth and value, lacking confidence, and overvaluing others while undervaluing oneself. It is NOT associated with entitlement, valuing one's rights over others, or taking what does not belong to you. Victims' self-esteem issues are generally *preyed upon* by offenders.

The link between esteem and aggression is complicated. One recent study showed that lower esteem helped prevent aggression following narcissistic provocation (Hart et al., 2019). In other words, men who experienced rejection and criticism and who did feel poorly about themselves were less likely to retaliate. Boldness, characteristic in many (if not all) sexual offenses, is correlated with narcissism and higher esteem (Miller et al., 2019). People with high narcissism and low esteem related to perceived rejection are more likely to endorse sexual coercion (Lamarche & Seery, 2019). It is the offender's narcissism, not self-esteem, that is related to offending.

A feeling of inadequacy or that the world is not making you feel good about yourself might lead to the idea that you deserve to feel better and will make yourself feel better at the expense of others. This is not low self-esteem. It is a result of narcissistic depletion leading to the right to self-indulgence. An offender might not have the power, influence, or admiration he thinks he deserves. It might be too difficult to impress an adult or fulfill the responsibilities of a healthy relationship. This is immaturity but does not cause sex offending. Offenders have intimacy issues, but offending necessitates secrecy and duplicity that destroy intimacy. It is not an intimacy deficit in the offender; it is egocentricity and superiority, as well as destructive behavior, that prevents him from being able to be close to his partner. Again, an offender may have interpersonal issues as a result of their challenging personality traits; these issues are not the cause of the offending.

Ascribing anger management issues to offenders is problematic as well. While a batterer or abuser might have anger management issues, the dynamics involved in abuse and intimate partner violence differ greatly from anger issues in other contexts. Anger is a minor component of intimate partner violence; control, entitlement, and egocentricity all play a much greater role (Bancroft et al., 2012). How does having an anger management problem explain how an offender can keep his cool at work, control himself until he gets into a private situation, or exact abuse in a cold, callous way? How can an offender be calm when the police get to the door when real anger is highly physiologically stimulating? Attributing an offender's systematic abuse to anger is short-sighted and can lead to missteps in an investigation.

"Why Do They Do That?" Pathways to Violence

Understanding how someone chooses to sexually assault or batter another person can be impossible, especially if that offender's actions are so foreign to our own values and experiences. We can assume, project, hypothesize, or invent reasons to explain an offender's choice to offend, all while missing the core elements that drive offense behavior. The abusive and assaultive acts are in service to the offender's need – that is the definition of instrumental violence. In offender-focused prosecution, identifying and understanding the needs of the offender, as well as understanding the offender's world view can open up avenues for investigation that might not be available otherwise. The offender has engaged in the crime but has also engaged in creating or organizing the environment to meet his needs.

Personality Traits and Intimate Violence

The strongest correlates to the commission of intimate violence, both sexual and physical, are personality traits that facilitate the commission of violence and abuse. There are two constellations of personality traits especially related to violence – antisocial and narcissistic traits. Antisocial traits include impulsivity, callousness, lack of regard for the rights of others, lack of remorse and empathy, and criminal-like beliefs that justify and rationalize destructive behavior. Narcissistic traits include grandiosity, entitlement, exploitiveness, and unreasonable demands for loyalty, special treatment, and admiration. These traits can overlap and converge to induce abuse and aggression in offenders. Personality traits like these distort the offenders' perceptions of self and others, giving rise to a worldview that allows abuse and diminishing internal barriers to intimate violence. Narcissistic traits, in particular, are related to repeated acts of violence (Barry et al., 2007; Hepper et al., 2014), while entitlement is a consequential risk factor in sexual offenders (Mann et al., 2010).

Antisocial Traits

Antisocial individuals do not conform to expectations of lawful behavior, are deceitful and impulsive, and are aggressive toward others. They lack remorse, an appreciation or concern for their impact on others, and empathy. Antisocial traits can be expressed as callousness and contempt, like in the offender who thinks, "The bitch was stupid enough to get drunk with me. What did she think was going to happen?" Victim blaming in offenders who abuse their partners is often fraught with callousness and contempt. She "poked the bear," "knows what I'm like," or "should have shut up when I told her to" are all examples of callous disregard, not only for the victim but also for the seriousness of the abuse itself.

Antisocial traits, like deceptiveness, callousness, lack of empathy, lack of remorse, low conscientiousness, and impulsivity, can exist in offenders without a history of criminality or criminal convictions. Many successful offenders hold antisocial beliefs and values while maintaining prosocial behavior. These beliefs may extend only to the offenders' household or be inhibited from being expressed outwardly because the offender understands the consequences. Even if the offender can generally recognize others' rights, his antisocial values can be activated when another person "deserves" what happens according to the offender's beliefs. This is evident in how offenders blame victims. A victim has no right to say no if she once said yes. If a victim gets the offender aroused, consent is not required. If a victim comes back or remains in contact with the offender, the victim's rights are abdicated. Again, when the offenders' antisocial beliefs or values are activated in a particular context or certain conditions, it meets their deviant needs.

Narcissistic Traits

Narcissistic traits are related to aggrandized egocentricity. The person with these traits can be arrogant, grandiose, exploitive, and entitled. They demand admiration, attention, and special treatment. People with narcissistic traits may feel above the rules and above others, their needs superseding the needs and rights of anyone else's. While the diagnosis of Narcissistic Personality Disorder is significant in offenders who batter their partners, commit mass shootings, and stalk (Bancroft et al., 2012; Eher et al., 2019; Metzi & MacLeish, 2015; Nijdam-Jones et al., 2018; Sorrentino et al., 2018). Even the presence of significant narcissistic traits is a predictor for violence and sex offending in an offender. Narcissistic reactions to sexual rejection were an impetus for sexual coercion (Baumeister et al., 2002). When the narcissistic individual is told no, he reacts with aggression and coercion to commit a sexual assault.

An offender's sense of entitlement is one of the strongest predictors of sexual and physical violence in offenders (Bancroft et al., 2012; Kjærvik & Bushman, 2021; Mann et al., 2010). Entitlement is the belief that one is warranted special treatment, rewards, and privileges without the reciprocity and responsibility that go with those things. The entitled person demands what has not been earned, wanting more than he rightly deserves. Entitled men perpetrate most violent offenses, including domestic violence and mass shootings (Bouffard, 2010; Madfis, 2014; Parkinson, 2017; Richardson et al., 2017). Entitlement can come from status, wealth, or real or perceived power. Offenders feel entitled to sexually or physically abuse others through a sense of ownership ("she was my wife/child"), as a reward ("I did a lot for these people"), or because of their own importance. "I mean, who was she to say no to me? She wasn't even that hot," an offender said. When an offender says, "I paid for dinner/provide for this family" or something like this, he asserts that he is owed. That precedes the right to retaliate or punish if he does not get what he thinks he deserves.

Exploitiveness and disregard for others are two other features of narcissism. Exploitiveness is the ability to take advantage of another person for one's own benefit. Offenders see vulnerability as weakness and opportunity. This includes the vulnerability of others who love and care for them. Intimate violence offenders monopolize the victim's attachment to them, using it against the victim to garner sympathy, protection, and dependency. They are adept at identifying people and situations to exploit and creating situations or states of vulnerability. Trust is a prime example. An offender will work to earn the trust of parents or a potential victim, only to exploit that trust for his own gratification. Along with an overinflated sense of self, narcissistic traits can entail the devaluation of others and a lack of empathy for others' suffering or pain. This trait is what allows an offender to torment his partner psychologically while she pleads for him to stop or explodes out of desperation and fear.

So many situations are ripe for exploitation – a victim's intoxication, dependency, love, disability, loneliness, and social isolation. What we blame the victim for in terms of making choices that made her vulnerable are the exact flashpoints that we focus on in offender-focused prosecution. The victim is blamed because she was drunk – who bought her drinks? The victim is blamed for staying with an abuser – who promised to change or get help. Who apologized? It is important to highlight the offender's exploitiveness rather than the victim's vulnerability.

Beliefs and Values of the Offender

Violent and criminal sexual behavior come from decisions, decisions based on a set of beliefs and values about the self, others, and the world. In examining narcissistic and antisocial traits, it becomes evident how these traits can create distorted beliefs about the world and the values that support these beliefs. An inflated assessment of one's own skills or rights can lead to beliefs that you deserve special treatment, that you are above others, and have the right to retaliate with violence if "provoked." Antisocial thinking, callousness, and exploitiveness lead to the idea that victims can "deserve what they get," that a violent or abusive response to the environment is rightly exacted. Entitlement and possessiveness, combined with the devaluation of others, can lead to the belief that other people are your possessions to do with what you want.

Violence comes from the combination of two primary beliefs – that violence or abusive behavior is an option and that the target deserves it. The offenders of intimate violence, whether sexual or physical, hold a set of constructs that allow them to rationalize and justify their behavior and accept the behavior as reasonable. Suppose an offender sexually harasses a soldier of a lower rank. In that case, his beliefs might include an acceptance of sexual domination, the idea that women should "expect" to be harassed in a man's world, and that the victim is asking for the abuse because she is too friendly. If an offender believes that hitting is an appropriate response to frustration, but hitting a supervisor is not an option, he may go home and hit his wife, who should have been more sympathetic to his frustration. All offenders of intimate violence accept that aggression, abuse, or sexually exploitive behavior is an option or reasonable choice when they justify it. When an offender devalues others or has a sense of entitlement to get what he wants when he wants it, it is easy to meet the conditions for abuse.

Offenders hold other beliefs as well. Offenders often have misogynistic beliefs that contribute to their violence and degradation of women. They may believe money, status, or rank bestows rights or privilege. The offender might have distorted values about sex based on pornography or warped ideas of love and devotion. There are an array of values that contribute to violence and abuse. Highlighting the twisted belief system of the offender can be useful in trial, especially if that offender has a public persona that hides these hidden convictions.

Sexual Deviance

This chapter will not explain sexual deviance. However, it is important to recognize that some offenders commit violent and sexual offenses because they are sexually gratifying for them. While not all offenders have a diagnosable sexual deviance, clinically called a paraphilia (e.g., pedophilia), all of the offenders who commit sex crimes have the capacity to remain aroused and get satisfaction in an atypical sexual situation. For example, an offender who rapes his partner can get and stay aroused despite the fact that his partner is crying, hurt, sleeping, unresponsive, and/or resistant. While arousal to the target or victim is not deviant per se, arousal in the context of the assault, including the risk of being caught or causing harm, is problematic. It is not "normal" sexual behavior to want to penetrate an unconscious partner who has vomited and urinated on herself. Facing the details of the sexual assault can help expose the aberrance of the offender's behaviors.

How Do They Do It? Methods of Manipulating and Influencing Others

Offenders have a powerful influence on the victims and their community. They want to offend and succeed at offending. Offenders are highly strategic at hiding their offenses. Very rarely does an offender commit a crime in the open, producing "hard" evidence and matching the stereotype of a creepy offender or a hypermasculine wife-beater. They have many means to manipulate the victim, as well as the community or "audience" to the offense. These are some common tactics to consider during the investigation and presentation of your case against the offender.

Picking and Crafting a Victim: Exploiting Vulnerability

Offenders choose victims specifically. Over and over again, offenders have described in treatment how they chose and then shaped their chosen victim. Offenders of children can spot a child who is quieter or has fewer friends than other children. Controlling offenders can test their victims to see who is more likely to be faithful or less confrontational. Victims' vulnerability takes many forms, including poverty, disability, intoxication, social or physical isolation, a prior history of abuse, mental illness, inadequate or missing social supports (like a single parent), or a poor reputation. Offenders choose vulnerable victims because they may also have credibility issues. Mentally ill and intellectually disabled people are at far greater risk of sexual and physical abuse than those without disabilities (Rossa-Roccor et al., 2020; Tomsa et al., 2021). They also are less likely to be considered credible or reliable witnesses.

Offenders may test the victims prior to assaulting or abusing them. In ongoing abuse, the offender generally crosses boundaries over time before escalating to more serious abuse. The offender who develops a pattern of assaulting his wife for years may have started by first verbally abusing her, grabbing her, or blocking her way. When she did not leave the relationship, he became emboldened to proceed. In one case of brutal rape, the victim's co-worker repeatedly threatened to kill himself. He found she would respond by coming to be with him, offering him support and comfort. The last time he did this, it was at three in the morning. He isolated her, then brutally raped her, asking "what did she expect," leading him on by constantly being there and leaving her husband's bed to be with him. These tests give the offender a great deal of information about the victim. The tests also are a component of grooming or the process of preparing a victim to accept the abuse.

Offenders create vulnerability in the victim as well, further prompting certain behaviors and reactions from the victim. There are overt physical and practical ways to create vulnerability in victims, like isolating or drugging them. But there are more insidious ways. Offenders are adept at getting the victim attached to them, like them, care for them, protect them, depend on them, and even love them. When an offender has intimate knowledge of another person, he can use that knowledge to cause self-doubt, low self-worth, dependency, and fears of abandonment in the victim.

Being Nice, Apologetic, Prosocial: Using Social Rules as Weapons

Humans are immersed in societal expectations of cooperation. When someone is nice to us, we tend to respond in turn. When someone apologizes, we are trained to appreciate and accept an apology. We are supposed to avoid conflict and confrontation; we are certainly not supposed to create it.

Offenders are keenly aware of social rules and the power of being nice. Niceness is an effective weapon against the victim. Being nice hides the true intentions behind behaviors. It shifts a demand of reciprocity onto the victim. For example, in a rape case involving a serial offender, victims willingly got into his car and accepted a ride home. He was the "nice" guy who acted as a designated driver for all his friends. He was pleasant and helpful. He would drive women home, women who trusted him and drank too much because they knew they had a ride. He would touch and photograph them while they slept in his car. He raped several. Imagine the immense task the victims had to confront him, to initially say no to his offer of a ride, especially when they knew he gave rides to others. Offenders understand how difficult it is to refuse or confront someone being nice to you. They understand the burden they create for the victim when they apologize for their actions, beg for forgiveness, or act confused by allegations, insisting it was a misunderstanding.

Offenders control others with the social rules they exploit. Social rules or social norms are the generally accepted guidelines for social behavior. They include saying hello in response to a greeting, shaking an offered hand, and being pleasant, helpful, and non-confrontational. There is considerable pressure to conform to these rules; many studies have been done on the power to conform (see, e.g., Zimbardo's (2007) book on the Stanford Prison Experiment). The offender is using all the rules for his own benefit. An offender will break all the social rules in the service of protecting himself. He will become offended by a reasonable question. He will personally attack the victim if she "dares" to question or challenge him. Offenders make reasonable people feel wrong for having concerns, wanting answers, or getting their own needs met. They make their victims feel terrible for calling out the abuse or offense. The victim has ruined them, broken their vows, or violated their privacy. The victim getting a divorce because of abuse is destroying the family and taking away the children's father. Social rules are the leashes that offenders use to control and manage victims; the victims are burdened with being the bad ones.

The Public Persona

One of the most effective manipulations is to create a public persona that others can believe in and think they can trust. Offenders can present in a highly prosocial and involved way. People around offenders are in disbelief when they find out about the offending. "But I know him," they will exclaim, "He wouldn't do a thing like that!" For some reason, people rely on this sense of familiarity with the offender to assume they know the offender's private or secret intimate behaviors.

Often the offender's public persona can contrast with the victim. The jovial co-worker can set up a situation to cause his "bitchy wife" to be confrontational and possessive at a work party. The people watching with sympathy for "what he has to put up with" have no idea that the man tormented his wife by degrading her sexually, saying he should trade her in for the woman at the office whose "ass wasn't so fat." The friends of the new father sitting at the bar whose "baby mama" tracks him down and screams at him have no idea he drank away the money for diapers. The police who arrive at the scene of a "domestic dispute" and encounter a hysterical victim telling them to leave have no idea that the last time they were called, she was anally raped as a punishment. Abuse and other intimate violence can produce symptoms in victims that the offender can use against the victim. A sexually abusive stepfather can complain about the problem child who will say anything to get him out of the house, who cuts and steals.

It can be easy for offenders to fool us by playing into biases, being nice, and becoming useful and valuable to people. Making people feel important works as well, stroking their narcissism. Understanding and using biases, stereotypes, rape myths, and misinformation about intimate violence is helpful to offenders. These tactics are beneficial to help the offender hide. They are highly effective in creating predictable victim responses as well.

Discrediting the Victim

Not only do offenders choose victims who have credibility issues but they also put active effort into discrediting the victims, often far ahead of any disclosures. The offender may spend months, if not years, smearing the victim to the outside world, either overtly or subtly. This discrediting appears in many forms, like telling people the victim is "crazy," portraying the victim as vindictive, or putting himself in a sympathetic light. It only takes a Google search on any allegation against a public figure to see how the victims become discredited. Offenders with status call reporting victims gold diggers. Discrediting the victim from the outset is very effective, especially when the public weighs in to judge an allegation. That public includes the players in the investigation and prosecution of intimate violence.

Using Fear

It is obvious that offenders use fear to control victims and their responses. The use of fear can be overt and obvious. Offenders directly threaten victims with viable consequences. Victims believe, rightly so, that they could be killed or further harmed by the offender. The offender uses threats of loss, isolation, poverty, or custody. The offender benefits from victims' fear of rejection, fear of losing love or family, or fear of reprisal from the community. Fear is one of the easier tools of manipulation to explain to juries when it is obvious. However, it is important to explore with the victim other less obvious fears that might have factored into the victim's decision-making. Having the victim explain the fears that the offender produced, both at the time of the offense and after, can be an essential component of the case.

Summary

As a society, we continue to maintain stereotypes and misinformation about offenders of intimate violence. You will have to confront these during your investigation and during your case. The misinformation impacts the victims as much as it does others; offenders exploit it to succeed. Offenders are expert puppet masters, controlling and engineering their environment to get away with countless crimes. They harbor character traits and distorted beliefs and values that facilitate their crimes. They are interpersonally astute, using us against ourselves and us against others to hide, deny, and camouflage their behaviors and intentions. Their behaviors have a profound influence on the victims, as well as on the players involved in your case. In conclusion:

- Misconceptions about the offenders and the causes of intimate violence need to be debunked in your cases.
- The violence perpetrated by offenders of intimate violence is instrumental, providing a specific gain for the offender.
- Offenders have problematic character traits that serve as a pathway to offending.
- Many excuses used by offenders are invalid as explanations of the cause of their instrumental, gratifying violence, including alcohol and acute mental illness.
- Vulnerability is not the fault of the victim. Vulnerability is only meaningful when there is danger. We must focus on the exploitation of vulnerability, not the fact that it exists.
- Offenders exploit basic social rules and prosocial behavior to carry out the preparation, actualization, and camouflage of their offending. We must be aware of this, so we are not distracted from seeing the offender for who he is.
- The victim can give you significant information about the offender and the manipulations he uses. Good interviewing about the context of the offending and offender's behavior can reveal information beyond the elements of the crime that help present the case fully to your jury.

References

American Psychiatric Association. (2013). *Diagnostic and statistical manual of mental disorders* (5th ed.). American Psychiatric Publishing.

Bancroft, L., Silverman, J., & Ritchie, D. (2012). *The batterer as parent* (2nd ed.). Sage.

Barry, C. T., Frick, P. J., Adler, K. K., & Grafeman, S. J. (2007). The predictive utility of narcissism among children and adolescents: Evidence for a distinction between adaptive and maladaptive narcissism. *Journal of Child and Family Studies, 16*(4), 508–521. https://doi.org/10.1007/s10826-006-9102-5

Baumeister, R. F., Catanese, K. R., & Wallace, H. M. (2002). Conquest by force: A narcissistic reactance theory of rape and sexual coercion. *Review of General Psychology, 6*(1), 92–135. https://doi.org/10.1037/1089-2680.6.192

Bouffard, L. A. (2010). Exploring the utility of entitlement in understanding sexual aggression. *Journal of Criminal Justice, 38*(5), 870–879. https://doi.org/10.1016/j.jcrimjus.2010.06.002

Davis, K., Kaysen, D., Gilmore, A., & Schraufnagel, T. (2013). Alcohol and sexual violence. In P. Miller (Ed.) *Principles of addiction*. Academic Press.

DeAngelis, T. (2021). Mental illness and violence: Debunking myths, addressing realities. *Monitor on Psychology, 52*(3). https://www.apa.org/monitor/2021/04/ce-mental-illness

DiBennardo, R. (2018). Ideal victims and monstrous offenders: How the news media represent sexual predators. *Socius*. https://doi.org/10.1177/2378023118802512

Eher, R., Rettenberger, M., & Turner, D. (2019). The prevalence of mental disorders in incarcerated contact sexual offenders. *Acta Psychiatrica Scandinavica, 139*(6), 572–581. https://doi.org/10.1111/acps.13024

Field, C., Caetano, R., & Nelson, S. (2004). Alcohol and violence-related cognitive risk factors associated with perpetration of intimate partner violence. *Journal of Family Violence, 19*, 249–253. https://doi.org/10.1023/B:JOFV.0000032635.42145.66

Giancola, P., Josephs, R., Parrott, D., & Duke, A. (2010). Alcohol myopia revisited: Clarifying aggression and other acts of disinhibition through a distorted lens. *Perspectives on Psychological Science, 5*(3), 265–278. https://doi.org/10.1177/1745691610369467

Grubb, A., & Turner, E. (2012). Attribution of blame in rape cases: A review of the impact of rape myth acceptance, gender role conformity and substance use on victim blaming. *Aggression and Violent Behavior, 17*(5), 443–452.

Hart, W., Richardson, K., & Breeden, C. (2019). An interactive model of narcissism, self-esteem, and provocation extent on aggression. *Personality and Individual Differences, 145*, 112–118. https://doi.org/10.1016/j.paid.2019.03.032

Heil, P., Ahlmeyer, S., & Simons, D. (2003). Crossover sexual offenses. *Sexual Abuse: A Journal of Research and Treatment, 15*(4), 221–236.

Hepper, E. G., Hart, C. M., Meek, R., Cisek, S., & Sedikides, C. (2014). Narcissism and empathy in young offenders and non-offenders. *European Journal of Personality, 28*(2), 201–210. https://doi.org/10.1002/per.1939

Kjærvik, S. L., & Bushman, B. J. (2021, May 24). The link between narcissism and aggression: A meta-analytic review. *Psychological Bulletin.* Advance online publication. https://doi.org/10.1037/bul0000323

Lamarche, V., & Seery, M. (2019). Come on, give it to me baby: Self-esteem, narcissism, and endorsing sexual coercion following rejection. *Personality and Individual Differences, 149*, 315–325. https://doi.org/10.1016/j.paid.2019.05.060

Lovell, R. E., Williamson, A., Dover, T., Keel, T., & Flannery, D. J. (2020, May). Identifying serial sexual offenders through cold cases. *Law enforcement bulletin* (official publication of the U.S. Federal Bureau of Investigation). https://leb.fbi.gov/articles/featured-articles/identifying-serial-sexual-offenders-through-cold-cases

Madfis, E. (2014). Triple entitlement And homicidal Anger: An exploration of the intersectional identities of American mass murderers. *Men and Masculinities, 17*(1), 67–86. https://doi.org/10.1177/1097184X14523432

Mann, R. E., Hanson, R. K., & Thornton, D. (2010). Assessing risk for sexual recidivism: Some proposals on the nature of psychologically meaningful risk factors. *Sexual Abuse: Journal of Research and Treatment, 22*(2), 191–217. https://doi.org/10.1177/1079063210366039

Metzi, J., & MacLeish, K. (2015). Mental illness, mass shootings, and the politics of American firearms. *American Journal of Public Health, 105*(2), 240–249. https://doi.org/10.2105/AJPH.2014.302242

Miller, J. D., Sleep, C. E., Crowe, M. L., & Lynam, D. R. (2019). Psychopathic boldness: Narcissism, self-esteem, or something in between? https://doi.org/10.31234/osf.io/5mfyr

Nijdam-Jones, A., Rosenfeld, B., Gerbrandij, J., Quick, E., & Galietta, M. (2018). Psychopathology of stalking offenders: The clinical, demographic, and stalking characteristics of a community based sample. *Criminal Justice and Behavior, 45*(5), 712–731. https://doi.org/10.1177/0093854818760643

Parkinson, D. (2017). Intimate partner sexual violence perpetrators and entitlement. In L. McOrmond-Plummer, J. Y. Levy-Peck, & P. Easteal (Eds.), *Perpetrators of intimate partner sexual violence: A multidisciplinary approach to prevention, recognition, and intervention* (pp. 44–54). Routledge.

Ramsey, C. (2015). *The stereotyped offender: Domestic violence and the failure of intervention.* https://scholar.law.colorado.edu/articles/56

Richardson, E. W., Simons, L. G., & Futris, T. G. (2017). Linking family-of-origin experiences and perpetration of sexual coercion: College males' sense of entitlement. *Journal of Child and Family Studies, 26*(3), 781–791. https://doi.org/10.1007/s10826-016-0592-5

Rossa-Roccor, V., Schmid, P., & Steinert, T. (2020, Sept. 8). Victimization of people with severe mental illness outside and within the mental health system: Results on prevalence and risk factors from a multi-center study. *Frontiers in Psychiatry.* https://www.frontiersin.org/articles/10.3389/fpsyt.2020.563860/full

Scurich, N., & Dietz, P. (2021). Psychological barriers to the detection of child sexual abuse. In D. DeMatteo & K. Scherr (Eds.), *The Oxford handbook of psychology and law.* https://ssrn.com/abstract=3786874

Simons, D. (2015, July). Adult sex offender typologies. *SOMALI Research Brief.* https://smart.ojp.gov/ somapi/chapter-3-sex-offender-typologies

Sorrentino, R., Brown, A., Berard, B., & Peretti, K. (2018). Sex offenders: General information and treatment. *Psychiatric Annals, 48*(2), 120–128. https://doi.org/10.3928/00485713-20171220-01

Tomsa, R., Gutu, S., Cojocaru, D., Gutierrez-Bermejo, B., Flores, N., & Jenaro, C. (2021). Prevalence of sexual abuse in adults with intellectual disability: A systematic review and meta-analysis. *International Journal of Environmental Research and Public Health, 18*(4). https://doi.org/10.3390/ijerph18041980

Ullman, S. (2021). Correlates of social reactions to victims' disclosures of sexual assault and intimate partner violence: A systematic review. *Trauma, Violence, and Abuse,* 1–15. https://doi.org/ 10.1177/15248380211016013

Zimbardo, P. (2007). *The Lucifer Effect.* Random House.

Chapter 3

What Made the Victim Act That Way?

Understanding Victim Response

She lay there naked, frozen, unable to move except to squeeze her eyes tightly shut, thinking that if she made eye contact, he would think she liked it. She repeated to herself that it must be an accident, he couldn't really mean it, maybe it was a new technique. And it was so quick. Then it was over. She sat up, numb and in disbelief. It was over. She got dressed. On the way out, she tipped him for the massage.

After he exploded because she did not pay enough attention to him at dinner, breaking a bottle and punching her in the head in the hotel room, he cried. He said he was drinking too much to "deal with the demons." She thought, "How horrible. He has so much trauma." He would go to treatment, he promised. Treatment was his way, he said, of "going the extra mile" to make their relationship work, to "make it different from the others." She made a commitment, deciding, "I've just got to love him more, show him I'm not going to go anywhere, he can depend on me."

Why didn't she scream out or get up when he assaulted her? Why on earth would she tip him? Wasn't that explosion a red flag? She could have gotten out early of a relationship that became months of hell. Why did she make excuses for him? Was she blind? How could she commit to someone who did that to her?

Victim response to intimate violence can be confounding, confusing, and counterintuitive, creating significant challenges during the investigation and throughout the prosecutorial process. Victims can act in ways that are frustrating, off-putting, and difficult to explain to juries, who continue to expect victims to act in predictable and expected ways. This chapter will explain that victim responses make complete sense *if you are open to understanding them*. Intimate violence, sexual or physical, requires a victim to make decisions in a traumatic, disorganizing context, fraught with complex feelings like disbelief, fear, betrayal, grief, and anger. Intimate violence is traumatic. Moreover, as we have discussed, its nature and reality are obscured by myths and misinformation, information that the victim has internalized, further muddied by the biases and feelings of the victim herself.

To understand what shapes victims' response to a violent, assaultive event, it is imperative to understand the entire context of that crime. While you may be investigating or prosecuting a crime, the victim has experienced numerous issues on multiple levels. That victim has had to rely on her understanding of herself, the assailant, and her world to best cope with being assaulted. To address faulty expectations of victim response in ourselves and others involved in the prosecutorial process, it is essential to consider all the factors influencing that person's decision-making

DOI: 10.4324/9781003121855-5

during and after the crime. What was going on inside the victim? What external issues were involved? And, most importantly, what was the offender's role in the victim's decisions and reactions? Below is a list of some internal, external, and offender influences on victim response. It is not a comprehensive list; asking the victim about her decision-making will provide information about issues that particular victim faced while undergoing the abuse.

Internal Factors

Trauma

Trauma is defined as the impact, psychologically and physiologically, of a highly disturbing or damaging event. Sexual assault, physical assault, and psychological abuse are all events that can produce trauma. The American Psychiatric Association (2013) characterizes a traumatic event as one that poses actual or threatened death, serious injury, or sexual violence. Terror, helplessness, the presence or lack of social support, the frequency and duration of the event(s), betrayal, and unpredictability all contribute to defining a traumatic event. Unmistakably, intimate violence can present all these issues.

Trauma can exist and affect a victim even if it is short-lived or does not result in a diagnosable disorder. And, there is no way to rate or rank trauma for another person, whether it is how much the victim was traumatized or what about the event was traumatic. Trauma is highly personal and may not result in what we expect. A victim may not be traumatized by being vaginally penetrated during a rape, instead having recurring nightmares of being forced to have the perpetrator's tongue in her mouth. A victim may not fear being hit but suffer more trauma from the psychological abuse, gaslighting, and threats she receives from her husband after she thinks things are "getting better." Studies contradict the belief that violent sexual assault causes more psychological harm than less violent assaults (e.g., Abrahams et al., 2013). Victim self-blame, a contributor to trauma and depression, is more significant in assaults that are less violent and more confusing to the victim (Kahn et al., 2003). Violent assaults are more easily identified as wrong, resulting in less victim blaming. In working with victims of assault, **never assume** the level of impact that a victim experiences from an assault of any type.

Trauma, Cognition, and Memory

The neurobiology of trauma and its impact on cognitive functioning is highly complex. The brain is full of structures that impact heart rate, respiration, memory, thinking, and behavior during an assault. The interactions of these structures are complex, unconscious, and reflexive. *What is simple is to understand that a traumatic event or threat floods the brain with numerous chemicals that affect how a victim perceives, decides, and remembers.* This flood of chemicals alters how the brain processes information, affecting multiple brain structures. These structures compete with one another and get disorganized, inhibiting the proper functioning in terms of memory formation and consolidation, thinking, and reasoning (Campbell, 2012; LeDoux & Pine, 2016; Schwabe, 2017).

The traumatic disruption in cognitive functioning impacts memory formation, encoding, storage, and retrieval. Traumatic events are associated with periods of forgetting or failure to recall the event at all, called traumatic amnesia, in a significant percentage of victims (American Psychiatric Association, 2013). Psychological defenses of denial, dissociation, depersonalization, and repression/suppression also impact memory. These defenses often disrupt the typical integration of cognitive function, including memory, perception, and behavior, following a traumatic event (American Psychiatric Association, 2013). The disorganization of the brain structures during a traumatic event can disrupt the encoding and accuracy of memory (Cozolino, 2017). Under trauma, the hippocampus, the structure of the brain responsible for organizing and encoding memory, can be less effective, resulting in fragmented or temporally disorganized memories. A victim might have missing pieces of events or remember them in a somewhat disorganized order (Schwabe, 2017).

This does not mean that a victim's memories are unreliable or fraught with inaccuracy. Stress and arousal may facilitate specific, long-lasting memories of salient and important elements of a traumatic event (Hoscheidt et al., 2014; Mathers & Sutherland, 2011). A victim may remember the details prominent to her or more details closer to the event while forgetting or never encoding more peripheral or less relevant details. Traumatic memory for details can be "burned in" someone's mind, a flashbulb memory. For example, a victim may vividly remember the perpetrator's smell or the time of the day while forgetting the order of events or what she was wearing. Recognize that the victim determines the importance of details. The victim may consciously focus on certain elements of the crime while actively avoiding attention to others. Multiple events like incidents of ongoing abuse can confuse peripheral details. In contrast, the victim may recall clearly and easily events with a unique element (an assault on Christmas Eve) that stands out to the victim.

Trauma compromises choosing and deciding as well. Thinking under stress is difficult. Trauma impacts our executive functioning, our higher-level decision-making, so we rely on ingrained behaviors and habits (Kozlowska et al., 2015), like the victims who report being on "automatic pilot" or going through the motions during or after trauma. Victims report being unable to think at all, confused, or focusing on seemingly "crazy" thoughts, like if she could get the kids to school on time. Planning an intervention or escape can be impossible. Then the victim might become exhausted after a trauma, unable even to consider productive action. This inability is referred to as quiescent immobility, occurring when the trauma is over and there is relative safety (Kozlowska et al., 2015), like when the rape is done, the victim falls asleep in the assailant's bed.

Course of Trauma and Secondary Victimization and Trauma

Trauma does not necessarily have a predictable appearance or course. Generally, trauma is thought of as acute or chronic. Acute trauma appears close to the traumatic event while chronic trauma endures over time. Trauma may have an impact on a victim during the assault. Alternatively, a victim might not develop trauma until well after the sexual assault or abuse. Trauma might not be a consequence of one event but a result of accumulated experiences. Trauma can be confounded by elements of love, betrayal, dependency, and vulnerability. Most victims of assault will not develop a diagnosable chronic trauma disorder. However, they will suffer with traumatic impacts of the assault on a subclinical level, like anxiety, depressive symptoms, intrusive memories, or intimacy disruptions. The development of trauma can come later when the victim can label the perpetrator's behavior. For instance, a child who cannot cognitively or emotionally appreciate the meaning of the sexual acts and behavior of the sexual offender might develop trauma as they mature, becoming better able to understand the abuse on a more advanced level.

This is one explanation for why a victim's presentation of trauma may change over time. The victim who laughed during the Sexual Assault Nurse Examiner (SANE) exam might be unable to talk without hyperventilating on the stand. The victim, who was incredibly distraught during the investigation but is emotionless when testifying, might be experiencing a lesser degree of trauma, having processed it in therapy. Trauma is not static.

Additionally, many victims experience secondary trauma or victimization due to the investigation or prosecutorial process. The events that follow a victim's disclosure can cause trauma, sometimes more than the assault itself. Negative experiences, like disbelief, lack of support, losses, or retaliation, can create trauma for the victim, impacting the victim's behavior. Secondary victimization by law enforcement decreases the likelihood that a victim will cooperate with the prosecution; the positive experiences of the victim are more likely to ensure a successful prosecution (Koster, 2016; Patterson, 2011).

Fear during the Assault

Fear, especially in highly threatening situations, is experienced psychologically and physiologically. When we are threatened, we react in a primal way, the goal being to survive and protect ourselves. The body responds physiologically to threat, activating several defensive reactions. It is essential to understand that the word fear does not differentiate the cognitive labeling of emotion from the innate defensive physiological response that occurs in the body (LeDoux & Pine, 2016). Our bodies respond to threats without the consciousness of the emotion of fear. Victims can experience post-traumatic symptoms in situations that are not frightening or react physiologically when they are supposedly "safe." For example, a victim of ongoing sexual harassment might become irritable, sweaty, or hypervigilant during a staff meeting the abuser is attending. She is having a physiological response to the threat without feeling fearful at that moment. Victims use words that do not reflect fear, instead explaining that they were confused, shocked, or uncomfortable. Fear is often not a response to coercive events or assaults when the victim is intoxicated, asleep, or unconscious. By understanding that the body's response to threat is automatic and unconscious, we understand that trauma can have an impact on a victim even when the victim is not consciously experiencing terror or fear.

The physiological impact of fear can produce misunderstood effects on victims' behavior, contributing to greater trauma, blame, shame, and feelings of helplessness. The first physiological response to a threat is to freeze. The freeze response effectively allows an opportunity to avoid being detected (like a prey animal in the brush) and gives time to process and assess danger. Freezing helps the body prepare for action (Roelofs, 2017). Freezing is usually an immediate but transient response. When the victim experiences shock or disbelief about what is happening, freezing can be more prolonged as the victim is unable to process the event. Victims will say they were "shocked," that their mind "went blank," or that they "shut down" during the assault. A victim who freezes might experience a profound sense of helplessness during the assault. "I was literally frozen," the victim explained when she awoke to find the perpetrator penetrating her from behind, "I tried to open my mouth to scream and nothing came out. I have never felt anything like that before. Then it was too late anyway." This feeling of helplessness can lead many victims to a diminished sense of competency, greater self-recrimination and confusion, and an amplified feeling of vulnerability. In extreme situations, a victim can experience tonic immobility. Tonic immobility, or rape paralysis, lasts substantially longer than freezing (Roelofs, 2017). Victims who experience tonic immobility are more likely to have post-traumatic symptoms, both men and women (Coxwell & King, 2010).

Fight or flight comes later as a response, sometimes only when it is too late. The assault might be finished, and the immediate threat is over. A sexual assault can be completed in the seconds or minutes it takes for the victim to appreciate or identify the event fully. Fight or flight can be mitigated by the victim's conscious decision-making, perhaps to submit, or take a different form, like a victim who seeks flight mentally by dissociating. Despite the conscious decision-making or behavioral outcome, the victim still experiences the physiological response to fear. A victim of a sexual assault described this, saying, "I just laid there. My heart was pounding so hard. I was sweating so badly that sweat was rolling down my ass." This victim had the physiological response to the assault while controlling her outward behavior – inside, she was panicking. Physical flight from a situation sounds simple but is very complicated. A victim must assess not only the situation but also the practicality and consequences of flight. An attempt to escape during an assault, or even after, might result in more severe consequences than the assault itself. It might trigger backlash from the perpetrator, bring attention from outsiders who could be problematic, or endanger others, like a child in the home. The fight response is even more unlikely during an attack. In a study focused solely on convicted rapes of victims by strangers, only 17% engaged in active physical violence, mainly kicking during the rape (Woodhams et al., 2011). When the victim has no strategy for fighting, a panicked response can be ineffective for self-defense (Roelofs, 2017).

The emotion of fear makes us overestimate the risk of harm, decreasing our likelihood of engaging in risky options like fighting back (Baron, 2007). Fear may cause an overestimation of the danger of resistance, an exaggerated assessment of the capacity for violence of the perpetrator, or feelings of peril when considering an unfamiliar behavior. A fearful victim may choose to submit, placate the offender, or "wait until it is over." We expect a victim to resist and fight an attack, but overcoming fear and acting self-defensively requires the development of habits for self-defense (Hopper, 2018), which most victims are unlikely to have.

Fear after the Assault

Fear impacts victims' reactions after the assault as well, potentially pervading decision-making well after the crime, especially if the victim has an ongoing relationship with the offender. Immediately after, the victim may fear antagonizing the offender by leaving, calling for help, or alerting the offender that the victim might take action. For long after the assault or abuse, victims might fear retaliation from the perpetrator or others for reporting or ending the relationship. They might fear that no one will believe them. The consequences of disclosure are a source of profound anxiety and fear for victims; sometimes, the victims fear being killed by the offender. This fear is justified – the greatest risk of being murdered comes at the dissolution of the relationship with an abuser. There can be many sources of fear or anxiety for the victim, all of which should be explored and acknowledged as affecting the victim's behavior. The fear of consequences and not being believed might arise immediately, overshadowing the assault itself. These are not unwarranted fears; studies show that not being believed, negative experiences with law enforcement or social supports, and the prosecution process can be more traumatic than the assault itself (Valliere, 2019).

Shame, Stigma, Humiliation, and Self-Blame

Victims of abuse and assault can experience intense feelings of shame, embarrassment, guilt, or self-blame. The very experience of being assaulted is confusing and humiliating, violating the victim's physical and emotional integrity. Shame, stigma, and self-blame are significant barriers to disclosure for both male and female victims, children and adolescents, victims of color, and LGBTQ+ victims (Calton et al., 2016; Lemaigre et al., 2017; Lowe & Rogers, 2017). Victims can feel self-blame or shame from believing they deserved the abuse, "allowed" it to happen, or brought it on themselves because of their choices. As we discussed, victims' feelings of shame and self-blame can be reinforced by the victim blaming in our society.

Shame, humiliation, and blame might arise during the investigatory process. The victim has to discuss deeply personal, intimate details of an event and her relationship with the perpetrator. Those things are examined in excruciating detail, over and over, with strangers who may not be kind, understanding, or careful. If the abuse is repeated, like in intimate partner violence, the victim has to relive numerous traumatic events or remember discrete details of each event. Each of these reports begs the questions of "why didn't you leave" or "why didn't you tell?" The shame of staying or loving the offender can be overwhelming in the face of judgment from others. Shame and self-blame play a significant role in labeling the experience as rape or abuse (Peterson & Muehlenhard, 2004), obviously impacting disclosure. The more blame a victim adopts for the abuse, the less likely the victim is to call it abuse and label herself a victim. In a relationship, the victim's shame may be about choosing a terrible partner, feeling that she provoked the abuse, participating in the aggression, or facing that this assault is not the first. An investigation of a sexual assault may include investigating the victim's sexual or other behavior. For example, a victim might have to describe how she knows the assault was different from the consensual times. "Well, I mean, we were into rough sex, it was our thing," the victim of rape said, "But this was different. He really hurt me on purpose."

Sexual response to an assault creates confusion and shame. If the victim responds physiologically to an assault, the victim might be confused about consent or the offender may claim consent as a defense (Levin & van Berlo, 2004). Orgasm, erections, genital stimulation, and lubrication can occur during an assault. A defense based on the victim's sexual response as proof of consent should be wholly dismissed (Levin & van Berlo, 2004).

It is essential to ask and explore with the victim what the victim believes she is to blame for and what she fears the investigator, prosecutor, or jury will blame her for. Not only will this allow accurate reassurance and intervention to occur but it will also allow the victim to explain this to the jury. Behavior becomes much more understandable in the context of fears and self-blaming beliefs.

Culture, Religion, and Socialization to Aggression

All victims are steeped in a culture and socialization that impacts their response to interpersonal violence. Victims have internalized beliefs, values, social rules, and customs that shape their interactions with their world. These include beliefs, values, and morals about gender roles, sex, sexuality, marriage, love, and aggression strongly influencing the victim's response to assault and abuse. A victim might be socialized to abuse or devaluation as a woman. A victim's culture might require that she protect the family or her religion require that she stay married. Culture and religion influence help-seeking behaviors – whom a victim should get help from and how outside resources are perceived. Victims might harbor cultural shame or cultural loyalty. Some subcultures distrust law enforcement and resist help-seeking, like undocumented victims or victims with addictions. Other subcultures dictate how the victim should report and to whom, like the military, that can take reporting out of the hands of an adult victim.

The culture or subculture of the victim can influence the investigatory process, prosecution, and jury decision-making. A soldier can be held to higher expectations of resistance and reporting. A sex worker's report of rape can be disregarded. A jury's perceptions of college life can disable their ability to understand sexual assault if they believe students often have drunk sex or that "hookups" are common. Investigators and prosecutors need to understand and attempt to navigate the issues of culture and religion with victims, both in order to have more effective rapport and to address these issues sensitively and proactively.

Disbelief, Confusion, or Denial

Because intimate violence is so profound and impactful, it is easy to assume that the victim easily identifies abuse and assault. This is not the case for either sexual assault or physical and psychological abuse. Victims are often unable to label their experiences as abuse, especially if the abuse does not fit their own internalized definition of abuse, those definitions often established in the same myths and misinformation maintained societally.

Initially, victims will experience disbelief that they were assaulted or abused. They report they were shocked, confused, or "just couldn't believe it." This is true even for chargeable crimes. A meta-analysis of over 5,900 victims revealed that more than 60% of rape victims failed to identify themselves as having been raped (Wilson & Miller, 2016)! Victims often label their abuse as something other than violence, whether it is sexual, physical, or verbal violence, calling it "bad sex" or "miscommunication" (Wilson & Miller, 2016). The disbelief can go on for quite some time. Not only does a victim have to understand that she was assaulted or abused but she also has to understand that the perpetrator is a person capable of the abuse. Marital rape or intimate partner violence can be especially confusing. The victim might believe she has no right to refuse sex or deny that the man she loves is that type of man. She might attribute his abuse to something external to him, alleviating his culpability for the abuse because he was drinking, depressed, or abused as a child. She may prefer to blame herself, saying she provoked him.

Numerous factors contribute to victims' inability to label their experiences as abuse or assault. Three of the more powerful are relationship to the perpetrator, use of alcohol, and presence of overt force or violence (Kahn et al., 2003). When a victim has a relationship with the perpetrator, the perpetrator has much more influence on the victim's perceptions and interpretations of the abuse, him, and herself. He can apologize, minimize, blame, or be indifferent. The victim is confused by the abuser's behavior. The victim might think it is a marital problem, an anger management issue, or an aberration for her spouse, who is "good down deep." Minimizing the abuse, reinvigorating dreams and hopes, and stressing the loss of the relationship and the abuser's willingness to change were identifiable tools used by the offender to get the victim to recant the allegations and attempt to drop charges (Bonomi et al., 2011).

Alcohol or drug use by the victim or perpetrator contributes to confusion and denial about abuse. When alcohol is involved during the time of the assault, a victim is less able to label the assault accurately. A woman who has been drinking might blame herself for "getting raped" or, if there was alcohol involved, might not label the attack as rape at all (Kahn et al., 2003). This finding was also true for whether or not the male assailant had been drinking.

If a victim believes overt violence is required to define rape or abuse, then "lesser" levels of attack or assault can contribute to a victim's confusion (Littleton et al., 2006). The rape myth that "real" rape is violent and forceful is also harbored by victims. When the offender is coercive or relentless but does not hit the victim or use a weapon, the victim might believe she was not "really" raped. A victim of physical and psychological abuse who lives in fear, walking on eggshells, might not believe her partner is abusive. Even being strangled might not hold the same meaning as being punched. "Well, it's not like he beats me," a victim will say, even though she has been "choked," shaken, and restrained. The victim could become more confused if she sees the offender's assault as a misunderstanding or her failure for not being "clear" enough. If the victim might have said yes but was raped while she was unconscious or very intoxicated, she might not label the experience as rape (Peterson & Muehlenhard, 2004). The victim may have flirted with or participated in sexual contact prior to the assault. She might excuse the offender's behavior. One study found that women who were perceived as sexually teasing "deserved" to be raped, and victims who saw themselves as teasing did not label their assault rape (Peterson & Muehlenhard, 2004).

Attachment to the Offender

Love is a powerful force. Loss of love is devastating – even when that love is destructive. Attachment to the offender is a potent force behind victims' response to assault and abuse. When a victim is attached to the perpetrator, she has to consider innumerable issues that complicate her responses during and after an assault. In intimate partner violence, a victim who reports has initiated a cascade of consequences upon herself and her love relationship. Loss, grief, practical and financial changes, and the knowledge that she is responsible for "punishing" her loved one are only a few of the actual considerations that accompany help-seeking. Loss is painful; change is frightening. Humans can experience loss twice as powerful as gain and pain more powerfully than pleasure (Brafman & Brafman, 2011; Kahneman, 2011). Loss is one of the most painful experiences of all.

The victim might be attached to the perpetrator through fear or dependency, as well as affection. The victim has experience with the offender and is "used to" the abuse, preferring the familiar to the unknown. The victim may fear what the offender can do if the status quo is disrupted. Practical concerns may keep the victim attached to the perpetrator, like finances or children. The victim may fear the unknown or fear what will happen if the offender is provoked but not contained. The victim may not trust the system to be proactive and protective, requiring her to strategize and optimize her safety. When the perpetrator has convinced the victim that she is responsible for the abuse and can control his behavior through hers, she may be attached to a false sense of power, believing that if she makes the right choices, she will be okay.

Any relationship with a perpetrator presents a complicated array of things the victim must take into account, along with the realization that the perpetrator assaulted her. If it is a boss, disclosure or reporting requires an assessment of risk – of job loss, retaliation, work upheaval. If a victim is being abused by her physician, she must consider being "redlined" as a patient, losing her access to care and drugs, or having to find another physician, which may be complicated by the doctor's specialty. If the perpetrator is an in-law, what happens to the family? If he is a priest, will he be believed and supported?

External Factors

External factors can compel victims' responses to violence as well. External factors are separate from internal influences, often outside the victims' control. Even if a victim is ready to report, seek help, or seek involvement in the criminal justice system, these outside forces or conditions can pose significant barriers for the victim, her choices dictated by social, economic, or practical realities.

Access to Services or Assistance

Access to services or help seems relatively simple to assess on the face of it. Often, a victim's failure to access service or get help is judged on a simplistic, superficial level during an investigation or trial. Why didn't she tell her doctor? Why didn't she scream, escape, or call for help? She had access to a car, went to work, saw her sister, then returned home without telling anyone she was assaulted. In reality, access to help can be highly complicated for the victim. An investigator uneducated about the complexity of this issue may fail to ask the right questions or may encourage the victim to endanger herself. Even victim advocates who cajole the victim into leaving or telling her family may unwittingly cause harm to the victim.

Investigators and prosecutors must explore the victims' actual access to services before concluding that the victim does not want help or want to cooperate. Does the offender read the victim's odometer, monitor phone calls, or accompany her everywhere? Is the offender closer to the victim's family than she is, friends with the local police, or the favorite soldier of the commander? Identifying the barriers to victims' help-seeking and access to services is crucial to understanding the victim and exposing the control and influence of the offender. Additionally, recognizing the victim's use of informal support is also useful. While formal supports include law enforcement and professionals, informal supports include friends, spiritual leaders, and family. These resources can provide information about the offender and history of the victim, and events that might be otherwise unavailable.

There may be easily identifiable practical reasons that the victim cannot access resources. The victim may not have access to money, have no driver's license, or be constantly responsible for childcare. The victim may have a language barrier or rely on the offender for citizenship. Victims in rural areas not only have limited services available but they may also fear a lack of privacy in a small community where the offender may be known to everyone (Logan et al., 2005). Victims in rural or tight-knit communities fear backlash. Male victims of intimate partner violence or sexual assault lack resources (Davies, 2002) as do members of the LBGTQ+ community (Calton et al., 2016).

Societal Response and Rejection

Victims fear and often experience a negative social response from formal (e.g., law enforcement) and informal (e.g., family) sources of support. Those negative responses include being blamed, disbelieved, confronted with skepticism, or dismissed. The fear of these experiences seriously hinders victim reporting and help-seeking when experiencing abuse and assault. A lack of social support not only makes a victim less likely to report but it also increases the likelihood that a victim will develop more psychological symptoms due to abuse or assault.

Victims' fears of adverse responses or social rejection are well justified. A meta-analysis of studies of negative social reactions to reports of sexual assault and intimate partner violence showed that formal support providers, like law enforcement, prosecutors, or professionals, are more likely to give negative social reactions than informal support providers (Ullman, 2021). This same analysis showed that Black and Hispanic victims, less educated victims, those who told sooner, and bisexual victims were treated more negatively, as were victims who blamed themselves more. Victims who were drinking were met with blaming, controlling, and stigmatizing responses. Even when seeking medical care, victims can encounter judgment and victim blaming. Nurses are more likely to blame victims if the nurse holds sexist attitudes or if the victim was raped by an acquaintance (Persson et al., 2018).

Negative Experience with Law Enforcement or Criminal Justice System

The National Domestic Violence Hotline did a survey in 2015 regarding victims' experiences with law enforcement, finding that victims of intimate partner violence demonstrate a "strong resistance" to utilizing law enforcement for help. More than one-quarter of respondents said they would not call the police, while half thought the police would make it worse. More than two-thirds thought the police would not believe them or do nothing (National Domestic Violence Hotline, 2015). Secondary victimization by law enforcement has been recognized for decades, but still occurs, as does secondary victimization by the court process. Victims of color, especially Black, face implicit criminalization because of their race, being judged "less innocent" than white victims (Epstein et al., 2017).

The prosecutorial or court process also offers its own sources of negative experiences. Prosecutors are prone to frustration, skepticism, and disbelief, as well. Cross-examination can be brutal for the victim, as can hearing allegations of lying, mental health issues, and vindictiveness. The process demands that the victim relive the abuse, recalling it in front of strangers. Following a report of abuse, a victim can face claims of parental alienation, efforts to control her, and undermining of her relationship with her children, in effect experiencing from the system what she experienced from the abuser (Laing, 2017).

Protection of Others

The need to protect others from knowledge or the consequences of reporting is another obstacle victims must overcome. This protection may be in response to a threat from the perpetrator who tells the victim he will kill her family or her pet if she tells. An adolescent might protect her mother from the knowledge that the stepfather is sexually abusive to save the mother's feelings or to protect the family from losing a provider. A victim of intimate partner violence may not disclose because the perpetrator has threatened their children, whether with overt violence or with "taking them" from the victim. There are many emotional and practical reasons a victim may have not to report or to return to the offender which involves protecting others. A soldier victim in a case did not disclose the abuse she was experiencing by the company's doctor while they were deployed because he was the only doctor there. She did not want fellow soldiers to lose a vital resource during a deployment.

Influence of the Offender

The offender is the most potent influence on the victim, especially when the offender and victim have a relationship. Time and time again, the victims' behaviors have been scrutinized in a vacuum during investigation and prosecution without any attention to the offender's actions. Victims' behaviors can easily be understood as normal responses to an offender's behavior in the abnormal context of abuse that the offender created. That is the primary reason for this book – to spotlight the offender's actions.

Offenders can manipulate the victim in very overt and easily identifiable ways. The offender can make a viable threat against the victim, using fear to dictate that victim's behavior. The offender can shame, humiliate, and blame the victim, using that victim's fear of social rejection against her. For example, a school teacher was abusing adolescent boys. He would get them to masturbate each other. By doing so, he ensured that they would not tell. The boys would be blamed, had demonstrated sexual arousal, and had engaged in behaviors with other victims. An offender can blame the victim for provoking, hitting, or sexually arousing him. The offender can punch the wall or demonstrate aggressive behavior around the victim to show his capacity for violence.

In cases of intimate violence, it is critical to understand how the offenders' actions manipulate and produce the victims' reactions and decisions. Many of these ways have been described in Chapter 2 of this book. However, a few deserve reiteration with some emphasis on how the behavior impels the victims' responses.

Love, Hope, Sympathy

Imagine the spouse you love, had children with, and have dreams about is sitting on the edge of your bed, crying. He is telling you all the things you have yearned to hear – it is not your fault, you deserve better, he knows now he really needs help, his own behavior confuses him, he will die if he loses you. Imagine the relief, the compassion, and the hope this generates in you. The promises and apologies empower you and activate you – there is something that you can do to stop the harm. You have value now.

Generating love, hope, and sympathy in a victim who wants a relationship gives the offender formidable power. Victims are typically bewildered by the actions of the offender. They search for reasons, excuses, and rationales to explain away the abuse or assault, anything to avoid the understanding that someone who was supposed to care for or love them would hurt and betray them. In order to seek prosecution against a perpetrator, the victim has to embrace values, feelings, and choices that might be in direct opposition to who that victim wants to be and has been taught to be. A victim of abuse must decide not to forgive, not to have empathy or sympathy, forego kindness and "second chances," and be that person who can tolerate seeing someone punished or incarcerated. Victims are blamed for ruining offenders' lives, careers, and families. A victim must eschew any feelings of responsibility, regret, or guilt to do this, which can be a Herculean task. This problem exponentially grows the closer the victim is to the offender. The attachment to the offender is the most important component of successful grooming, according to the abused children interviewed in one study (Katz & Barnetz, 2016). As discussed, offenders are keenly aware of the need to build a relationship with their victims to control them better. A relationship with the victim makes that victim vulnerable to manipulations and fear of loss of the offender.

Identifying and Exploiting Vulnerability

Offenders are highly adept at identifying and exploiting vulnerabilities in their victims. These vulnerabilities might include physical or psychological limitations, like mental health issues. The victims might have personality traits that make them more vulnerable, like shyness or insecurity. The victim might struggle with addiction, poverty, a prior history of abuse, or a poor reputation. The victim might be especially kind, naïve, or trusting. A victim might be difficult, challenging, or behaviorally problematic, already having a pre-existing reputation as a "liar" or "troublemaker." All these vulnerabilities make it more likely that the victim will be receptive to the offender's attention, as well as be deemed less credible when she makes allegations.

Offenders can make a victim more vulnerable over time. Not only can the offender make the victim love or care for him but he can also socially isolate the victim from friends and family or create financial dependence. Having children together makes the victim more vulnerable. An insidious example is the offender who brutally beat his wife for months. She already had a complicated relationship with her dysfunctional family. He formed a group text with her family members, of which she was not a part. He would tell them private things about her or claim she said things against them. He complained and cried about her behavior. She became more and more estranged from her family. He beat her so badly that she escaped by jumping on a flight with her head still bleeding. Eventually, she had little help or support from her family, and he alienated and frightened her friends. When she tried to leave, she was alone.

An offender can also create and exploit vulnerability at the time of the offense. An intoxicated victim is vulnerable if she is taken to his place at 3:00 a.m. without a car. The offender can withhold food or medication. He can bring more drinks to an already intoxicated person. He can be the designated driver for the group, taking the victim home while leaving her friends at the club. Focusing on the offender's exploitation of the vulnerability rather than the vulnerability will help keep victim blaming at a minimum.

Counterintuitive Behavior

We can acknowledge that we have expectations of how "real" victims act, as faulty as these expectations are. However, we also have internalized expectations of how "real" offenders look and act. It is certainly not acting "normal" or like nothing happened. Who is acting more in line with expected behavior – the child obediently responding to the adult in charge or the stepfather masturbating openly while asking the child about school. The child has to pretend that nothing is happening, while the offender acts like nothing is.

Offenders act in a way to confuse the victim. Most often, the offenders act like nothing at all happened, behavior that is very disorienting to the victim. The offender who snuggles up to the victim he just raped and kisses her goodnight has now completely obscured his actions and intentions. The batterer who gets up the next morning and cheerily greets the spouse he verbally abused until 3:00 a.m. has confounded the victim's sense of what happened. The guy who just forced his penis into the college girl's throat in the bathroom, who exits the bathroom yelling loudly about doing a beer bong, cannot be the same person who just committed a felony. Outsiders to abuse and assault look for signs the offender is "like that" in his public behavior, as much as they judge the victims and their expected responses. Offenders are good at engaging in behaviors that counter this for the victim and everyone else.

Grooming the Community

Not only does an offender use techniques to confuse and manipulate the victim but they also groom the community. The offender can manipulate the outsiders or audience to the abuse in the same way that he can the victim. Offenders produce disbelief and doubt about the victim and construct a public persona that shields others from knowing them and understanding their capacity for violence and harm. An offender who is calm, cordial, and pleasant to all the members of the church he attends weekly will be given significant credibility when he denies allegations of abuse, asserting that he is "not like that!" The husband who never gets angry at any family function may be defended by the victim's mother, who says, "He is never that way with me! You must push his buttons." Recently an offender insisted to me, "Ask anyone I have ever worked with – I am the most even-keeled person they know! No one has ever seen me get angry. They all know I couldn't have done a thing like that!"

Offenders can control the audience's information, especially in an environment where the offender is supported and involved. For example, an offender may go to work and "confide" in his boss or manager that he is having marital problems, that his wife has a drinking problem, and thinks she might have a boyfriend. When the offender tells his boss that his wife has accused him of abuse, he can say sadly, "I should have seen this coming. She wants to take the kids and house and have her boyfriend move in." Offenders can offer plausible explanations for situations or circumstances. The offender who shows all his friends the sexting he did with the victim prior to the allegations is proving information that will form their opinion of whether or not the victim "really wanted" it.

The offender can easily diminish the victim's credibility by controlling information and using a public persona to establish himself. Time and time again, offenders will immediately offer that their accusing wives are bipolar or vindictive. They might even tell on themselves, admitting to "cheating, which was so wrong," but being undeserving of such extreme retaliation as being accused of rape. The more an offender can highlight the victim's issues or portray the victim as problematic, the more likely the victim's allegations will be dismissed. A negative portrayal of the victim can also prepare the offender's supporters to retaliate against the victim. The social media attacks on professed victims during high-profile trials are vicious, based on perceived vindictiveness and the alleged offender's sympathetic presentation.

Summary

Victims' behaviors and reactions to intimate violence are a product of a myriad of influences, internal, external, and, most importantly, the offender. A victim's behaviors are almost always understandable and explainable if you adopt the stance that victims act normally in an abnormal context. As society learns more about victimization, we have improved our recognition and response to the effect of victimization and understanding victims' psychology. But there is a long way to go.

Intimate violence is disorienting, disorganizing, and damaging. The scrutiny and demands that follow reporting are incredible. The investigation process can be as or more traumatizing than the assault itself, including the intrusive experience of a sexual assault examination. However, a greater understanding of victim response can be achieved through education and confrontation of faulty expectations. Offender-focused prosecution can help accomplish this. As we improve, victims will be more likely to come forward and cooperate, resulting in more successful investigations and prosecutions of abuse. In conclusion:

- A multiplicity of factors affect victim behavior – internal, external, and offender-produced.
- A reasonable investigation will assess all the factors that impact the victims' behaviors without making assumptions.
- Trauma is a component of intimate violence that alters victims' experiences in ways that affect the investigation and prosecutorial process.
- Victims face multiple barriers to reporting and cooperating with an investigation or prosecution. These barriers can be minimized by providing a forum for curiosity and understanding while avoiding judgment and devaluation of the victim.
- An offender-focused investigation and prosecution require an exploration of the offender's influence on the victim, including what the offender knew and exploited about the victim.
- Violence has an enduring impact, producing diagnosable symptoms of the trauma and creating alterations in the victim's perceptions and experience of the world.
- An offender-focused prosecution requires a full understanding of the victims' world-view and the offenders' influence on the victims' response. Explaining these dynamics effectively in court will spotlight the offenders' role, effectively assisting your prosecution.

References

Abrahams, N., Jewkes, R., & Mathews, S. (2013). Depressive symptoms after a sexual assault among women: Understanding victim-perpetrator relationships and the role of social perceptions. *African Journal of Psychiatry*, *16*, 288–293. https://doi.org/10.4314/ajpsy.v16i4.39

American Psychiatric Association. (2013). *Diagnostic and statistical manual of mental disorders* (5th ed.). American Psychiatric Association.

Baron, J. (2007). *Thinking and deciding* (4th ed.). Cambridge University Press.

Bonomi, A. E., Gangamma, R., Locke, C. R., Katafiasz, H., & Martin, D. (2011). "Meet me at the hill where we used to park": Interpersonal processes associated with victim recantation. *Social Science & Medicine*, *73*, 1054–1061.

Brafman, O., & Brafman, R. (2011). *Sway: The irresistible pull of irrational behavior.* Doubleday.

Calton, J., Cattaneo, L. B., & Gebhard, K. (2016). Barriers to help-seeking for lesbian, gay, bisexual, transgender, and queer victims of intimate partner violence. *Trauma, Violence, & Abuse, 17*(5), 585–600. https://doi.org/10.1177/1524838015585318

Campbell, R. (2012, December 3). "The neurobiology of sexual assault." *An NIJ Research for the Real World Seminar,* National Institute of Justice: US Department of Justice. https://www.nij.gov/multimedia/presenter/presenter-campbell/Pages/welcome.aspx

Coxwell, A., & King, M. (2010). Adult male rape and sexual assault: Prevalence, revictimization, and the tonic immobility response. *Sexual and Relationship Therapy, 25*(4), 372–379. https://doi.org/10.1080/14681991003747430

Cozolino, L. (2017). *The neuroscience of psychotherapy: Healing the social brain.* W. W. Norton & Company.

Davies, M. (2002). Male sexual assault victims: A selective review of the literature and implications for support services. *Aggression and Violent Behavior, 7*, 203–214.

Epstein, R., Blake, J., & Gonzalez, T. (2017, June 27). Girlhood interrupted: The erasure of black girls' childhood. https://papers.ssrn.com/sol3/papers.cfm?abstract_id=3000695

Hopper, J. (2018, September 5). Why it's time for sexual assault self-defense training. *Psychology Today.* http://www.psychologytoday.com

Hoscheidt, S., LaBar, K., Ryan, L., Jacobs, W. J., & Nadel, L. (2014). Encoding negative events under stress: High subjective arousal is related to accurate emotional memory despite misinformation exposure. *Neurobiology of Learning and Memory, 112*, 237–247. https://doi.org/10.1016/j.nlm.2013.09.008

Kahn, A., Jackson, J., Kully, C., Badger, K., & Halvorsen (2003). Calling it rape: Differences in experiences of women who do or do not label their sexual assault as rape. *Psychology of Women Quarterly, 27*, 233–242. https://doi.org/10.1111/1471-6402.00103

Kahneman, D. (2011). *Thinking fast and slow.* Farrar, Straus and Giroux.

Katz, C., & Barnetz, Z. (2016). Children's narratives of alleged child sexual abuse offender behavior and the manipulation process. *Psychology of Violence, 6*(2), 223–232. https://doi.org/10.1037/a0039023

Koster, N. (2016). Victims' perception of the police response as a predictor of victim cooperation in the Netherlands: A prospective analysis. *Psychology, Crime, & Law, 23*(3), 201–220. https://doi.org/10.1080/1068316X.2016.1239098

Kozlowska, K., Walker, P., McLean, L., & Carrive, P. (2015). Fear and the defense cascade: Clinical implications and management. *Harvard Review of Psychiatry, 23*(4), 263–287. https://doi.org/10.1097/HRP.0000000000000065

Laing, L. (2017). Secondary victimization: Domestic violence survivors navigating the family law system. *Violence Against Women, 23*(11), 1314–1335. https://doi.org/10.1177/1077801216659942

LeDoux, J., & Pine, D. (2016). Using neuroscience to help understand fear and anxiety: A two-system framework. *American Journal of Psychiatry, 173*(11), 1083–1093. https://ajp.psychiatryonline.org/doi/pdf/10.1176/appi.ajp.2016.16030353

Lemaigre, C., Taylor, E., & Gittoes, C. (2017). Barriers and facilitators to disclosing sexual abuse in childhood and adolescence: A systematic review. *Child Abuse and Neglect, 70*, 39–52. https://doi.org/10.1016/j.chiabu.2017.05.009

Levin, R. J., & van Berlo, W. (2004). Sexual arousal and orgasm in subjects who experience forced or nonconsensual sexual stimulation. *Journal of Clinical Forensic Medicine, 11*, 82–88.

Littleton, H., Axsom, D., Breitkopf, C., & Berenson, A. (2006). Rape acknowledgement and postassault experiences: How acknowledgment status relates to disclosure, coping, worldview, and reactions received from others. *Violence and Victims, 21*(6), 761–778.

Logan, T., Evans, L., Stevenson, E., & Jordan, C. (2005). Barriers to services for rural and urban survivors of rape. *Journal of Interpersonal Violence, 20*, 591–616.

Lowe, M., & Rogers, P. (2017). The scope of male rape: A selective review of research, policy and practice. *Aggression and Violent Behavior, 35*, 38–43. https://doi.org/10.1016/j.avb. 2017.06.007

Mathers, M., & Sutherland, M. (2011). Arousal-biased competition in perception and memory. *Perspectives in Psychological Science, 6*(2), 114–133. https://doi.org/10.1177/1745691611400234

National Domestic Violence Hotline. (2015). *Who will help me? Domestic violence survivors speak out about law enforcement responses.* http://www.thehotline.org/ resources/law-enforcement-responses

Patterson, D. (2011). The linkage between secondary victimization by law enforcement and rape case outcomes. *Journal of Interpersonal Violence, 26,* 328–347. https://doi.org/10.1177/0886260510362889

Persson, S., Dhingra, D., & Grogan, S. (2018). Attributions of victim blame in stranger and acquaintance rape: A quantitative study. *Journal of Clinical Nursing,* 1–10. https://doi.org/10.1111/jocn.14351

Peterson, Z., & Muehlenhard, C. (2004). Was it rape? The function of women's rape myth acceptance and definitions of sex in labeling their own experiences. *Sex Roles, 51,* 129–144.

Roelofs, K. (2017). Freeze for action: Neurobiological mechanisms in animal and human freezing. *Philosophical Transactions of the Royal Society B, 372,* 20160206. https://doi.org/10.1098/rstb.2016.0206

Schwabe, L. (2017). Memory under stress: From single systems to network changes. *European Journal of Neuroscience, 45*(4), 478–489. https://doi.org/10.1111/ejn.13478

Ullman, S. (2021). Correlates of social reactions to victims' disclosures of sexual assault and intimate partner violence: A systematic review. *Trauma, Violence, and Abuse,* 1–15. https://doi.org/10.1177/15248380211016013

Valliere, V. (2019). *Understanding victims of interpersonal violence: A guide for investigators and prosecutors.* Routledge Press.

Wilson, L. C., & Miller, K. E. (2016). Meta-analysis of the prevalence of unacknowledged rape. *Trauma, Violence, and Abuse, 17*(2), 149–159. https://doi.org/10.1177/1524838015576391

Woodhams, J., Hollin, C., Bull, R., & Cooke, C. (2011). Behavior displayed by female victims during rapes committed by lone and multiple perpetrators. *Psychology, Public Policy, and Law, 18*(3), 415–452.

Section II

Building a Better Case
Offender-Based Evidence and Practice

Chapter 4

Building Your Case

From the very start, successful offender-focused prosecution relies on the foundation upon which the case is built. You must build your case on the idea that it is the offender, not the victim, who is being prosecuted. This starts from moment one.

The Paradigm Shift

From the beginning of these complex cases, law enforcement and prosecutors make the mistake of apologizing for the victim's choices, finding ways and relying on assumptions to defend the victim. Why concentrate on the victim's behavior? The question should not be, "Why does she stay with the abuser?" The question should be, "Why is he hurting her?" Instead of asking why she was alone with him, ask why he ignored her when she said no. This shift of focus changes our perspective on all the issues we will see in the case before us.

Once we begin to build our cases in an offender-focused manner, we start on the offensive, not the defensive. We can successfully adopt the belief that any behavior of the victim that is "counterintuitive" can, and rightly should, always be blamed on the offender. She stayed? That is because she is afraid, truly believes he will take the children, or, worst of all, thinks he will change. The victim has a substance abuse issue. She can explain she is self-medicating to survive an emotionally and/or physically abusive relationship. She had an affair. Is it no wonder that someone who is told she is worthless and not loveable day after day may find solace in someone who treats her with love and dignity? These questions must be asked, of course. We need to know the answers from the victim, who then can explain how the offender's behaviors dictated her behaviors.

Once we realize where the focus should be – on the offender – we can open the file and look at it in a different light. This will require a paradigm shift in the way you approach cases.

Recognizing the Impact of Myths

The biggest challenge with investigating and prosecuting intimate violence is that we live in a society that does not understand the dynamics of victims' reactions to being assaulted. The myths surrounding intimate partner violence (IPV) and sexual assault (SA) are more prevalent than ever. These myths lead to bias, misunderstanding, and, worst of all, judgment on every single level of the criminal justice system, from first responders through trial and even sentencing. As a result, it can take just one person in the process (unintentionally, we hope) to affect a victim's decision to participate in the prosecution of the offender.

DOI: 10.4324/9781003121855-7

Anyone who has done this work for a substantial amount of time knows there are "Oh sh★t" moments as they investigate the case, moments are when you are asking yourself, "Why?" Why did the victim not resist? Not scream out? Minimize? Not report? Stay in contact with the rapist? Recant? If you look deeply enough and ask the right questions, you will find that the victim's explanations make perfect sense. Law enforcement and prosecutors are just as vulnerable to believing intimate violence myths as any other person. The danger is that it leads to judgments about a victim's credibility, and this misplaced judgment may have a chilling effect on the victim wanting to participate or, worse, a decision not to move forward with charges when they are warranted.

Starting Right, Right from the Start

Building a case requires laying a foundation. The foundation must be built on a solidly constructed relationship with the victim, as well as firmly held beliefs about who is the defendant and who is the victim. This requires immediate decisions for law enforcement and prosecutors to approach the case thoughtfully, with the pitfalls of bias and misinformation in mind.

Follow-Up

The most significant mistake law enforcement and prosecutors can make is failing to follow-up with the victim close in time to the complaint/arrest. We assume that if a victim says she will cooperate at the beginning of the process, she will continue to cooperate. As discussed earlier, the victim is influenced by the behaviors and intentional manipulations of the perpetrators at every turn. Prompt follow-up by law enforcement could reap better photographs, more detailed narratives, and even the discovery of the offender's attempts to obstruct justice. Bruises appear and may worsen in the days after an assault. The offender will engage in calling or texting to try to gain control of the situation. The victim finds that she urinated on herself during a strangulation, something she notices when she cleans up her clothing. All these new findings can be used in a future prosecution of the offender even if the victim does not cooperate at trial. On a similar note, prosecutors reaching out as soon as possible could be much more successful in developing rapport, increasing the chance of keeping the lines of communication open when the victim is making critical decisions. Rapport building will be discussed in much greater detail later in this book.

Thorough Analysis of Challenges, Questions, Assumptions, and Missing Information

My practice as a prosecutor is to read the complete investigative file AND TAKE NOTES. I look closely for all the things my experience tells me I need to address, question, or clarify. I take a separate legal pad (I am that old) and write down all the "issues" or challenges in a case. These include, but are not limited to:

- What a Judge or jury will question, given that it is likely that they adhere to myths about intimate violence?
- What the victim did or did not reveal during the first interview?
- What questions are unanswered or were unasked?
- What witnesses were not identified or included?
- What is needed to corroborate a victim's account?
- What action steps are needed immediately to preserve evidence?

The victim will not always reveal everything in an original interview, depending on the interviewer's skills and the victim's comfort level. We must remember that law enforcement approaches things from a probable cause standpoint, so there are questions or areas that law enforcement may have pursued. These include names of witnesses mentioned in an interview that law enforcement may not have spoken to yet. Commonly missed witnesses include first responders, child protective service investigators, health care providers, neighbors, roommates, other family members, or the victim and offender's friends, family, and confidants.

The next step is to critically think about the questions that need answering or follow-up. This includes not only what questions need to be asked but also how to ask them. Confronting a reluctant victim with accusatory questions that feel like an interrogation can immediately derail a victim's cooperation with an investigation. A "wish list" is useful, setting down evidence that would ideally corroborate the victim's account. These include things like the offender's phone, social media, closed circuit television (CCTV) footage, or other things that would require action for preservation. The list could include any communication between the victim and the offender prior to or following the assault, the victim's medical records, or social media posts. I will be discussing potential evidence more comprehensively in Chapter 6.

The offender's law enforcement interview can be a gold mine. Watch the interview closely – even if he or she invokes. Pay special attention to the portion of the offender's interview when the officer is out of the room; you may see and hear things that will help. If there is no video of the interview, carefully review any written interrogation of the offender. Even a denial or claim of consent can be useful later as more details are revealed. Watch or read every victim and witness interview closely. Information from one may be helpful in guiding follow-up interviews with others. Lastly, review the available digital evidence. Review everything as thoroughly as possible before the initial substantive interview of the victim, so you do not have to continually go back and ask further questions.

Charging Decisions

Deciding whether to file charges can be difficult, especially in special victim cases. These crimes are mostly committed in private. The offenders know the victims and create behaviors in victims that diminish the victim's credibility when she does not act like she is "expected" to act.

As a best practice, begin with two questions. First, what were the circumstances of the report? The circumstances of when, where, why, and to whom can be very telling. For instance, if a SA victim does not report for a month, then decides to report when she sees the offender exhibiting similar behavior toward another woman, that can be compelling. Her motive is protection of others. It is very common for victims to report because they fear someone else could be victimized. Similarly, an IPV victim may not even have intended to report, but a neighbor or bystander calls the police. Her report is unintentional, but made when she finally feels safe to report or scared enough because now the neighbors know. The second important question involves the purported "motive to lie." If the supposed motive to lie can be invalidated, it makes the charging decision easier. For instance, a commonly cited motive to lie for victims in IPV cases is that there is a divorce pending. This is easy to explore and discredit. Was the violence ever alleged in the divorce? Does alleging abuse even impact a divorce? In many states it does not because they are ruled by no fault divorce laws. The most logical answer is that divorce is not a motive to lie about the abuse. She is divorcing him because he is abusing her. Ironically, we constantly tell victims to leave a toxic relationship, but when they do we use it against them, accusing them of fabricating the abuse.

Summary

From the start of the case, from the moment the investigation begins or you open the case file with all its challenges and complexity, you must adopt an offender-focused approach. This requires a paradigm shift where we stop defending the victim and start prosecuting the offender. Offender-focused prosecution relies on confronting and dismissing myth adherence, recognizing the need to quickly establish a connection to the victim, and identifying the appropriate issues that will fill in the blanks or corroborate the victim's accounts. Learning to ask about and explore the actions of the offender must start from the very beginning. A clear perspective from the beginning will guide the case throughout the process.

Chapter 5

Building a Relationship with the Victim

In cases of intimate violence, the most important thing a prosecutor can do is build rapport with the victim. The victim's account forms the backbone of the case; that is the bottom line. Every other witness or piece of evidence must corroborate the victim's account or refute the offender's anticipated excuses. As a prosecutor, your relationship with the victim can make or break the direct examination, generally the centerpiece of a criminal case. You can lose an intimate assault case with a credible victim, but you cannot win a case of intimate violence with a victim who does not seem credible. The prosecutor's relationship with the victim is the lynchpin to determining how the victim performs on the stand during a potentially painful direct.

The How

How do you develop a good relationship with the victim? It can be challenging, especially given that the victim has been harmed by someone trusted, through a relationship and vulnerability, the exact situation you will be hoping to establish. Despite this, there are some basic steps to take that establish you as different from someone harmful, perhaps even a prior investigator or prosecutor.

The Introduction

Few things cannot be repaired or addressed in terms of forming a relationship with the victim. The introduction is one of them. The investigator's or prosecutor's initial response to a victim anchors that victim in her experience of the process. Remember, as we have discussed, initial negative reactions to the victims from law enforcement or anyone in the prosecutorial process can be the sole determiner of whether or not a victim cooperates with the investigation. Frustration, dismissal, disbelief, or skepticism are all adverse reactions that powerfully impact the victim. The prosecutor or investigator can address problematic issues later and successfully with victims who initially experience support and acceptance by the prosecutorial team.

The prosecutor and involved investigator should introduce themselves to the victims early, as soon as possible, to outline their roles in the process and give the victim as much information as possible. It is easy to lose sight of the fact that the criminal justice system is a mystery to those outside it. Victims are often confused, expect things to move very quickly, or rely on television portrayals to understand the process they are entering. For many of us, it is our life. We become immune to the life-changing impact of our day-to-day jobs. The victims' lives have changed when they become involved with the criminal justice process, no matter the outcome. Having some information, even basic information, like who has what role, can be tremendously reassuring.

DOI: 10.4324/9781003121855-8

One initial thing that is safe to say to every victim you speak with is, "I am very sorry this happened to you." This statement conveys to the victim that you care about them as a person and are interested in more than just gathering facts for the case. For the longest time, prosecutors were taught that the first thing to say to a victim is that we believe them. Victims have taught us that this might not be the best first thing. For example, in one case, a detective interviewed a child victim of sexual assault. The detective was comforting and supportive, telling the child that he wholeheartedly believed him. The boy became distraught, then insecure. It had never occurred to the child that he would not be believed. Since then, I no longer say this to victims unless they tell me someone did not believe them or they fear not being believed.

Ensuring or Enhancing Victim Safety

In cases of intimate violence, the prosecutorial team must take steps to address victim safety issues. Not only will this go a long way to establishing rapport and trust with the victim but it will also help ensure that the case goes forward and the threat of harm is minimized. If you do not address the victim's safety issues, that victim may be worse off than the day before she met you. This concern is especially true in intimate partner violence, when the victim may have to return home with the abuser.

You must assess the victim's situation. Is there a protective order in place? Is there contact between the victim and perpetrator through children? Does the victim feel in jeopardy at the moment? The prosecutor or someone on the team needs to be familiar with resources, like shelters, and be able to have the victim explore her own support systems for safety. Remember that the victims who present to you after an assault may be disorganized and have difficulty planning. Even asking questions about safety is important to show how seriously you are taking the victim's situation. Obviously, the prosecutor cannot be solely responsible for the victim's safety. Still, someone on the prosecutorial team should know what needs to be asked and what can be done to make the victim safer. The first is to ask the victim how imminent (if at all) she feels danger is. Victims can be very astute in predicting the abusers' behaviors. Second, someone on the investigation or the prosecution team, like a victim advocate, should be familiar with two important tools for enhancing safety: A lethality assessment and a safety plan.

Lethality or Danger Assessment

First responders should perform a danger or lethality assessment with the victim, an assessment which should be performed throughout the prosecutorial process. The lethality assessment is a short list of questions the victim answers that identify factors associated with a greater risk for lethality in intimate partner violence. Developed by Jacquelyn Campell in 1985, this assessment is designed to identify factors associated with a greater risk for the victim of being killed by the perpetrator. It can easily be downloaded from www.dangerassessment.org and used readily. It assesses issues related to escalation, use of weapons, and offender factors that negatively impact the victim's safety. A higher score indicates a higher risk of being seriously harmed or killed, something that an investigator, advocate, or prosecutor can use to educate and motivate the victim to seek greater protection.

Safety Plan

A safety plan is a plan for victims comprised of a set of actions they can take to lower their risk of harm and enhance their safety. It includes strategies for escape, items the victim should have on hand, and resources the victim can utilize. An interactive safety plan can be found here: https://www.thehotline.org/plan-for-safety/create-a-safety-plan/. A simple Google search can produce many examples of these plans as well.

While a prosecutor might truly wish for a victim to leave the offender or at least not reside with her abuser, this may not be possible. A safety plan allows a victim to look to the future while acknowledging the risk she is currently experiencing. Even asking about a safety plan or introducing the victim to the concept can be extremely helpful and empowering. Often, a victim is only told to leave. This advice can make the victim feel hopeless, misunderstood, or burdened by the responsibility to take action she does not want to or cannot take. A safety plan acknowledges the process of leaving, the need for the victim's safety to be paramount, and a recognition by the prosecutor of the victim's situation. Given that many victims of intimate violence have multiple contacts with law enforcement before being able to get free from the abuse, a prosecutor who appreciates the complicated situation the victim is in and is concerned with her safety is more likely to see that victim if she is assaulted again.

The victim's safety must be the number one priority. In addition to the victim's physical safety, the prosecutor must also consider the victim's emotional safety. To reiterate, the victim must have emotional and psychological safety during the process. Does she trust the system? Does she trust that the prosecutor believes her and will not judge her? This emotional safety can be as important as a victim's physical safety in prosecuting the case and allowing that victim to speak her truth.

Supporting the Victim

Developing a good relationship with the victim is supporting the victim. Support is in the form of providing an atmosphere of respect and curiosity for the victims. Your job is not to rescue or befriend a victim. You need to remember your role and respect these boundaries. But you need to create an atmosphere that offers the victim what you can in terms of respect, consistency, and information.

Most prosecutors have great respect for victims. What they might not have is the ability to communicate it or to remain aware of what it is like on the other side of the work we do. It is so difficult to wait with the unknown, rely on people who are unknown to you, and be involved in an inscrutable system. Ask yourself – what is my communication style? People have different ways of communicating, and some can be off-putting. If you are an all-business personality, you may come off as stiff and uncaring, even though the exact opposite is true. Perhaps during introductions, you explain to the victim that your focus and intensity mirror your dedication to the case but say you also care about the victim's feelings. Help the victim not to take your style personally. Say that you understand how difficult it may be to talk about the assault. Find your communication style to give information and get information so the victim can make informed choices. But make it authentic.

This author's style incorporates humor and levity. It may seem strange, considering the seriousness of the subject, and these are very serious crimes. The humor and levity I use are self-deprecating, my way of trying to break down barriers that a victim might feel because of my position or their basic fear of being judged. For example, when I meet a victim for the first time, I will introduce myself, tell them I am sorry this happened to them, and then tell them three things about myself. I offer information to humanize me, not to share deeply personal information. For instance, I might joke about being a "natural" redhead who needs to be "refurbished." I might say something about my favorite college sports team, which is weird because I did not attend that college. I want the victim to see me as a little more "regular" than the prosecutor, who will sit and ask about the most terrible thing that happened to her. I also invite the victim to ask questions during the process, so she feels like a part of it. For instance, if she needs clarification or needs help understanding why we are asking something, she can get an explanation.

This style might be different from your style. Many prosecutors are uncomfortable sharing anything personal, feeling this blurs professional boundaries. It may be confusing for some victims. This is not advice to model, just an example of being comfortable with yourself in a very difficult situation. In all situations, finding something personalizing the interaction between you and the victim is helpful. It communicates that you are a person and that the victim is not just a witness in a case. Acknowledging something about the victim, like that you noticed where she grew up, can help. Simply stating the obvious might be the most helpful – this is really tough, and you will try your best. If she needs a break, ask for one. Is she nervous? Make sure you have tissues available. Support is not grand action; it is a presence that means that the other person matters.

To be comfortable with your style, you have to become comfortable with talking about abuse and assault. If you are queasy or hesitant to use sexual terms or talk about sexual things, the victim will also be. If you are sensitive to language and how a victim describes the assault, the victim may feel judged. For example, one victim who was brutally raped was reprimanded when she said, "Then that motherfucker put his dick in my pussy!" The interviewer told the victim she should not use "that language." You can imagine how the rapport disintegrated.

Educating and Informing the Victim

It is tempting to tell the victim things, to announce the way forward, and to dictate advice. This can be especially true if the victim presents in a confused or vulnerable way. However, it is better to help the victim understand what you are looking for and provide information to make informed choices – about what information to provide and what decisions to make during the process. Though it can be a shortcut when you need patience, dictating information without informing or educating the victim can replicate the controlling dynamics of abuse.

Victims do not know what they need to tell. They might focus on the "crime" or presenting event. They might not think what they have to say is important or "part of the case." They might reveal too much, finally free to speak openly about the abuse and recount everything that ever happened. Victims are unsure what details are important or unimportant, especially if the responding officers predetermined their understanding of the case or the process!

A potent tool for interviewing victims is the Power and Control Wheel (https://www. thehotline.org/identify-abuse/power-and-control/), developed by the Domestic Intervention Project in Duluth, Minnesota. It is a readily available and often used tool that outlines the tactics used by abusers with their partners. Sitting down with a victim to review each component, and asking whether the partner used them on the victim, can be a valuable way to get information from the victim while educating her about the types of things you are looking for in your interview. Not only does it provide information for the victim but it also reveals your familiarity with the entire experience of intimate violence. Victims have asked, "How do you know my husband?" This experience with you can lead to an in-depth conversation about the fact that abusers act so consistently in terms of social, financial, physical, and emotional abuse experts were able to create this wheel to show how common these behaviors are. This is a powerful message to the victim that she is not alone. It is also a profound and necessary message that you are offender-focused, not focused on blaming her. You are saying that it is not her fault but the fault of the abuser.

Managing Expectations

Educating the victim means educating the victim about the process. Victims, or the general public for that matter, do not understand the slow and tedious wheels of justice. From the beginning, explain the steps in the process. Explain how long an investigation might take and what information needs to be attained. Discuss why there might be a continuance. Outline some of the rights the defendant has during pre-trial and trial. Give the victim a sense of how many interviews might be necessary, what travel is involved, and who will be the contact for her if she has questions. Do not overpromise or over-commit. And stay in touch throughout the process with the victim. This does not mean daily phone calls – it means letting the victim know you are still aware she is out there waiting. You need to inform her of delays and developments. Far too often, these authors have seen victims go for months, even over a year, with no contact about the case from the prosecutor. Their motivation to participate wanes. On the other hand, simple acts like a prosecutor who makes a quick call to see how someone is or to say happy birthday have a powerful impact on the victim's attitude and cooperation, even if the case drags on much longer than anticipated. Managing the victim's expectations is critical to supporting and fostering the relationship with the victim.

The Importance of Empathy

Empathy is the ability to share or experience someone else's feelings, to see and experience the world from another's point of view. The mistake we make with empathy is putting ourselves in someone else's shoes. However, the key to genuine empathy is to *be someone else in their own shoes*.

The things that victims fear most from the criminal justice system are being judged and not being believed. The most dangerous thing that prosecutors can do is attempt to put themselves in their victims' shoes. Why? We can easily believe that we would not have acted the same way the victim did. We would have left. We would have fought back. This is not empathy. Empathy is gathering information about the other person and understanding how and why that person made the decisions they did. We are in danger of judgment and blame if we somehow put ourselves in the victim's position. Because we would have done something different, ascribing ourselves strengths and resources we think we have, the victim is at fault for her choices. True empathy reveals that, ultimately, none of us know how we would react if sexually assaulted or abused by an intimate partner. That is the level of openness and blamelessness we must have to show victims empathy.

Empathy can be very difficult, especially when we sincerely cannot understand another's position. You cannot fake it; victims can see right through that. And, frankly, victims can be very challenging to work with, especially if you have become the source of their anger and fear. If you have investigated or prosecuted intimate violence for any significant period, you have been yelled at, told you are horrible, told to mind your own business, and cursed. This hostility can be hard to take, especially when you come from a place of caring. You must remember that these victims are doing everything they can, every day, to survive. Maybe you are a safe place for the victim to vent her frustrations about the system and how she has been treated, even the abuse itself. You cannot take it personally. I have had victims who tell me they hate me and hoped I would die, only later to thank me for being one of the only people in their lives that has ever stood up for them. It is a process, and it is not an easy one.

The best way to show empathy is to make eye contact and give a victim your full attention. Listen carefully. Ask relevant questions. Finally, you can simply state that you have no idea what the experience was like for her. But that you want to know. Do not try to find some common ground about vulnerability that might be inaccurate. Only say what you truly can empathize with — that the assault is completely disruptive, frustrating, terrifying, or unimaginable. What you say matters. How you say it matters even more, which will be discussed at length in the next chapter.

Summary

Building stronger victims builds stronger cases. If the victim is comfortable on the witness stand and she trusts the prosecutor asking the questions on direct examination, she will be able to convey her truth in an authentic and compelling manner. A strong relationship with the prosecutor affords the prosecutor the ability to directly ask the victim about behaviors, decisions, or situations that the defense might otherwise use to discredit the victim. When a victim trusts the prosecutor, she will be able to answer questions about why she did not tell, went back, had sex with him after the rape, or acted as if nothing happened without the fear of judgment. The victim will be better able to explain herself to a judge or a jury when she feels like she is not being asked the questions by someone wanting to humiliate her but by someone who wants others to understand, too.

Your relationship with the victim is the vehicle to this safety. Establishing rapport can make or break your relationship with the victim. If you can establish trust, the victim will feel supported during the process. You do not have to agree with the victims' choices. You have to push your biases aside and fight for the victims unapologetically. In conclusion:

- Your relationship with the victim is a powerful prosecutorial tool. It starts in the beginning, with your introduction and willingness to understand.
- A relationship should be offered at the beginning of the case and maintained throughout the process. Simple steps and missteps can profoundly impact a victim's cooperation.
- Find your style. Become comfortable with the language and subject area. If you have a style that is hard for people to read, let the victim know that upfront.
- Attend to the safety and support of the victim.
- Educating, informing, and managing expectations can foster your relationship with the victim.
- An offender-focused approach facilitates a strong relationship with the victim. The victim is an ally and resource who does not feel blamed or judged but is empowered to provide information that solidifies the case.

Chapter 6

Offender-Focused Investigation

Every prosecutor's case starts with and relies upon the investigation. The prosecutor decides whether to go forward based on the evidence presented at the outset. Charging decisions depend on the investigation, its completeness, and its focus reliant upon the law enforcement investigators who complete it. The prosecutor must have a good working relationship with their law enforcement, beginning with providing law enforcement information and training on offender-focused case construction.

Working with Law Enforcement

While it may seem evident that a criminal investigation should be focused on the offender, law enforcement, particularly the first responding officers, can be problematically focused on the victim. As we have discussed, law enforcement may make immediate decisions on the victim's credibility or motive to report based on bias and misinformation. They may make problematic conclusions or assumptions about the offender, especially if the offender seems "cooperative." They can decide inaccurately about who the aggressor is based on visible wounds.

It is the prosecutor's job to clearly communicate the expectations of law enforcement and educate them about an offender-focused investigation. The prosecutor cannot simply rely on, then be disappointed in, the investigators' uninformed decision-making. Law enforcement officers are subject to excessive demands, frustration, and the stress of dealing with victims and trauma. If the prosecutor has not explained the "why" behind the prosecutor's expectations and requirements, investigators might feel burdened rather than as an essential part of the prosecutor's case. Explaining why evidence is critical and how it assists the prosecutor can go far in garnering the investigators' efforts for better offender-focused investigation.

Three main topics need to be discussed with law enforcement to make an investigation optimal. The first is how to identify, collect, and preserve evidence properly. The prosecutor should provide information on what kind of evidence the prosecutor wants to be collected and what evidence is essential in offender-focused cases. When the investigators understand why the evidence is important, they are more likely to focus on it. Recording demeanor can provide the prosecutor, then fact finder information that can identify the victim's distress and trauma. For example, if the investigator documents the victim's cognitive disorganization, it might corroborate the victim's claim that the offender strangled her. However, if the investigator does not understand the need for clear documentation, this evidence might be lost by an investigator who decides at the scene that the victim is "crazy."

Secondly, law enforcement needs to be trained in determining who is the predominant aggressor in a crime of intimate partner violence. When victims can be hysterical, angry, or aggressive

DOI: 10.4324/9781003121855-9

at the scene, the investigator might immediately decide that she is the problem, especially if they are untrained in identifying defensive wounds. Often defensive wounds are immediately visible, while evidence of other injuries appears later, like bruising. Many victims are still being arrested because law enforcement is not properly trained in understanding intimate violence and what constitutes a primary aggressor.

Finally, the prosecutor should give law enforcement basic information on the rules of evidence. This might include explaining an excited utterance, what is necessary to overcome hearsay, or other basic principles. For example, a prosecutor can stress to law enforcement the need to document direct quotes from the victim. However, if you do not explain WHY those quotes are important, they may not understand their importance of them. Evidence can be lost.

The Window of Opportunity

Law enforcement and prosecutors should recognize and embrace that in crimes of intimate violence, there might only be one window of opportunity – the initial contact with the reporting victim. First responders have the best chance of getting the most information from victims of intimate violence. This initial contact, often during a time of escalation and crisis, will provide the window of opportunity to get the most information for the investigation, possibly information that will never be available again, especially if the victim does not want to cooperate in the future.

When first responders arrive on the scene of a recent assault, the victim is accessible. The victims are safe, surrounded by helpers. The victims are distraught, angry, afraid, and unfiltered, feeling the immediate impact of the assault before the feelings fade. Additionally, the offender has been separated (hopefully) from the victim or is in custody, so is unable to manipulate or, worse, threaten the victim. The investigation at the scene must be thorough, and the follow-up with detectives must be swift. In general, police are taught to make initial reports short and simple. However, in intimate violence cases, the more information included in the report, the better it is for the case.

Victims often become uncooperative in cases of intimate violence, especially when the offender gains access to the victim. The victim may recant within days of the incident or the first court appearance if she even appears. Law enforcement should be trained that the investigation of these cases does not end with the offender's arrest. Follow-up with the victim should repeatedly occur, after 24, 48, and 72 hours. This follow-up can achieve two goals. First, it provides an opportunity to take supplemental pictures to show an injury that might not have been visible at the scene, like swelling and bruising, which may develop over time. Second, it is an opportunity for investigators to inquire about any intimidation attempts by the offender, which could lead to additional charges such as violation of a protective order or obstruction of justice. Knowing that an offender has attempted to influence the victim can be critical to the prosecutor, alerting the prosecutor that the offender is interfering in the investigation.

Advice for First Responders

In working with first responders, there are a number of effective rules of thumb that a prosecutor can provide. The prosecutor can tell first responders that there can never be enough information, but there can be too little. Good information begins with *good* contact information for the victim. This does not simply mean the victim's cell number but also the contact information for person she talks to most often. A victim can easily avoid or block calls. Access to an important member of the victim's support system may give you a chance to reengage her in the process. The prosecutor can get information from that support about what the victim is struggling with or questioning. It allows the team to counteract the lies the offender is telling the victim or demystify the prosecution process. Putting effort into remaining in contact with the victim signals to the victim that the assault is important, as is her well-being.

Prosecutors should explain to first responders that getting the complete history of past interpersonal violence is as important as documenting the fullest version of the event they are investigating. The offender's history of abusing the victim can provide information about the relationship, the offender's reach over the victim, the duration of the abuse, and the potential investigation of other chargeable offenses. The investigators should ask who the victim has told about the abuse and when, especially in proximity to the current offense. Then, the investigator or detective can ensure a follow-up with that potential witness.

First responders must understand the importance of documenting direct quotes and the victim's demeanor. Immediate documentation of quotes becomes important for a few reasons. First, the average first responder answers hundreds of calls a year. Getting a case to trial can take substantial time, a year or even more. It is improbable the officer will remember what the victim or offender said. If the statement is not documented precisely, the responder may inaccurately remember, sometimes complicating a case or making it appear that the victim has been inconsistent. With a properly documented quote, the officer does not have to remember what either party said. The records have it.

An officer is more likely to be diligent in documentation when the officer is mindful of the importance of the evidence. The prosecutor can explain that a victim's statements in quotes and demeanor can become significant at trial as an excited utterance. An offender's quoted statement can be useful, whether that statement is inculpatory (implicating) or exculpatory (clearing) regarding the allegation. It seems counterintuitive to put an offender's exculpatory statements in the report, but it may be helpful later. For example, an offender might say, "I never touched her," or "she fell down the stairs." Yet the victim has an injury. At trial, when the medical evidence refutes the claim that the victim fell down the stairs, the offender will have to change his story. He must offer an alternative explanation for the injury. The officer should understand that it is equally important to document the offender's demeanor. If he is raging on the scene, telling the victim to "shut up" or threatening her, he may be charged with other crimes. It is undoubtedly helpful to expose the offender's rage to the jurors at trial. If he is calm and cool, claiming to the officer that the victim is "crazy and a drunk," that is equally as revealing. The prosecutor can incorporate his presentation into the theme and theory of the case.

Other Sources of Evidence: The Urgency Involved

There are many sources of evidence that will disappear if not collected as soon as possible. Proper and accurate documentation of the crime scene through diagrams, photos, and videotapes will be unavailable if not done immediately. A victim's or offender's willingness to give consent to obtain records, screenshots, medical documentation, or social media information may dissipate over time, resulting in a loss of potentially critical evidence. Collecting and acting on these consents should be done urgently, as evidence can be lost if the victim changes her mind. In too many cases, we have seen that the offender offers his phone at the time of the crime, only to have it refused by the responding officers. Unsurprisingly, this phone is unavailable, broken, or erased after the window of opportunity has closed. Surveillance evidence, like CCTV and Ring camera footage, may have a short shelf life.

When law enforcement does request access to the parties' cell phones and social media, they may have access to a gold mine of evidence. At the very least, the responding officers should obtain screen shots of texts that corroborate the victim's version or inculpate the offender. This evidence can be pivotal if the victim decides not to participate in the prosecution later. Even if the evidence itself is not collected, the officer can get information on what the victim and offender use, like Facebook or Instagram, or where relevant information might be, like texts, emails, or voice mail. Then the prosecutorial team can immediately send out preservation letters that protect the information from destruction. An actual voice mail or text message is the evidence preferable if the officer can get them.

Other things that need to be obtained quickly are 911 calls and phone records. While the actual messages are preferrable, phone records can still be corroborative. The phone records may not show us the actual text messages or content of a phone call, but can prove that there was an actual text or phone call placed. Records can also help to disprove any defense attempts to allege that the victim "spoofed" a call or text.

Spider Web Investigations

Spider Web Investigations are commonly used in investigating narcotic distribution but are very useful in investigating crimes of intimate violence. In this type of investigation, the investigator would track the targeted main supplier to uncover others connected to the target. In cases of intimate violence, the investigator can focus on the offender's current victim, then branch out to former wives, girlfriends, friends, and co-workers. In the military, the offender's prior assignments and stations can be investigated. Offenders of intimate violence are generally serial offenders, likely to have other victims. The investigation may find these victims, which can reinforce and corroborate the case. Even if barred by the statute of limitations, these other victims and crimes can still be utilized as 404(b) evidence.

Summary

Taking the time to discuss with law enforcement about the importance of initial and follow-up investigations can be the difference between an acquittal and a guilty verdict. The key is not just to tell them what you need but to explain why you need it that way. First responders must understand that the collection of as much evidence as possible during the window of opportunity significantly helps strengthen the prosecutorial case. An offender-focused prosecution relies on an offender-focused investigation. In conclusion:

- There are valid reasons a prosecutor wants a report written a certain way or why specific evidence needs to be collected immediately. Share those reasons with your law enforcement team.
- Prosecutors should explain why an offender-focused investigation will always be more beneficial than an investigation that questions the victim's choices. An approach that judges or blames the victim increases a victim's distrust of the system and the likelihood the victim withdraws from the prosecutorial process.
- Working with first responders not only helps ensure that they get what the case needs but also affirms their role's importance. Crimes of intimate violence are often a source of frustration and helplessness for law enforcement, who see these cases "go away" over and over despite their efforts.
- An offender-focused approach to investigation spearheads the prosecutor's ability to present an offender-focused prosecution.

Chapter 7

Offender-Focused Interviewing

Offender-focused interviewing is a strategy for interviewing that is twofold. First, it assists the investigator and prosecutor in founding the case against the offender and getting as much information about the offender as possible. Second, it establishes with the victim a way to get information that minimizes judgment and blame, decreasing the victims' reluctance to share and increasing the level of rapport and trust between the victim and the prosecutorial team.

General Issues and Recommendations

First, though we are making recommendations about the course and content of an interview, it is imperative to *be flexible*. Some basic interview strategies will work for most victims, but there are always exceptions. The most important thing to keep in mind is that victims should be able to proceed with an interview in the manner that is most comfortable. Typically, law enforcement and prosecutors become goal oriented during interviews, trying to identify and gather the information that will help get an arrest and guide charging decisions. We like to receive information chronologically and linearly – a "just the facts" approach. While this is ultimately necessary, it is problematic for victims of intimate violence. The victims' experiences are chaotic. The salient, important "facts" are personal, not "criminal." Trauma impacts memory and disclosure. There is not usually, for the victim, an available chronology of events that the victim can narrate in a linear fashion. A skill interviewers need to develop is the tolerance for a bit of chaos that they can later revisit and clarify. It also helps to have a competent note-taker always present in interviews!

Your goal in the first interview should not be to get all the details of the assault, even though you may feel an urgency to do so. The victim needs an introduction – to you and the players in the prosecutorial team. The first interview is a chance to get to know each other and to outline the process for the victim. However, if the victim wants to dive immediately into the details of the assault, do not miss the opportunity. Some victims feel an urgency to tell, something that may decrease their anxiety. Let them do so, being prepared to tolerate the possibly disorganized narrative you are offered. However, most victims are uneasy delving straight into the assault.

Think about where you want to do the interview. Prosecutors may consider allowing the victim to decide where that first interview should occur. While your office may be convenient, it may be difficult for the victim. Imagine the gigantic desk between you and the victim, with all your credentials displayed, perhaps even pictures of your happy family. It can be very intimidating. Choosing a more comfortable or neutral place might work more effectively to show the victim you can meet her on her terms or at least consider her comfort. Rapport building can become much easier.

DOI: 10.4324/9781003121855-10

It is essential to be accessible to the victim and convey that you see her as a person, not just a victim. Remember, the assault brings you together, but it is not everything that the victim is. Getting the victims to talk a bit about themselves helps put them in an emotionally neutral place and gives you something to refer to in the future, showing you are interested and this is not just a "case" to you. We need to have some insight into their lives outside the crime. Knowing that the victim's son has baseball practice can allow you to acknowledge this when you have an interview – "I remember the afternoon might not be good because of Sam's practice." Also, making sure that the victim knows to and is allowed to ask questions should be established from the beginning.

The Goals of the Interview

In an offender-focused prosecution, the goal of the offender-focused interview is to identify the facts and issues relevant to the prosecution of the offender. Obviously, you must gather the elements and facts about what happened to the victim. But you cannot stop there. It is vital to learn to ask questions that reveal the offender – how he influenced the victim's behaviors and responses, how he set up the crime, and what he did to ensure his needs were met, including preventing reporting.

The main goal of a substantive interview is gathering information that leads to corroboration. Seemingly insignificant details make all the difference in rebuilding memory, re-creating the reality of the crime, and supporting the victim's account of the crime. During the interview, the victim's descriptions and disclosures can guide further evidence collection, identify other witnesses, or provide intimate information about the offender that will be useful during the case.

Second, the substantive interview is the time to understand and decide how to deal with any "counterintuitive" behaviors that inevitably come with intimate violence cases. The victim (with the right questions) can begin to explore her reasons for not immediately reporting, what made her recant, or what made her decide to have sex with the offender again after he raped her. An effective offender-focused interview will help the victim identify many offender behaviors and influences and understand that her decisions made sense or could be explainable instead of shameful.

Lastly, you must identify all potential charges and other bad acts that may not be chargeable but may be presented to show the offender's motive, plan, or abuse of the victim, otherwise known as F.R.E. 404(b) (described below). From the outset of your case, identifying other "bad acts" is crucial in crimes of intimate violence, particularly intimate partner violence, when the abuse has been ongoing. While the offender's verbal abuse and psychological maltreatment might not be chargeable, it has had a profound impact on the victim. It is almost always influential in dictating the victim's behavior during or after the abuse, creating the challenging, "counterintuitive" behavior that has to be explained to uneducated juries. Knowing these acts and being prepared to argue for their introduction at trial arms the prosecutor for trial.

Setting the Stage

With any interview of a potential victim, it is imperative to set the stage. The victim comes to your interview with no idea how the process works. To form rapport, it is important to inform and educate the victim and put the victim at ease. You need to explain the interview's purpose and address the victim's immediate concerns. You need to explain that the purpose of the interview is to gather evidence and to make sure that the victim is being understood, not blamed or judged.

Remember, law enforcement comes from a very different place than prosecution does. When law enforcement does an interview, they gather evidence to determine what crime was committed and determine whether there is probable cause to arrest. The prosecutor's role is highly different. The prosecutor's burden is beyond a reasonable doubt. Therefore, the questions should be quite different. Law enforcement needs to understand what happened. The prosecutor must explain what happened, how, and why.

One of the most essential things prosecutors must do is adjust their expectations of the victim and the interview. The victim will not have answers to every question for various reasons. Sometimes they are not ready to answer. Sometimes they genuinely do not know. Sometimes they are not equipped psychologically and emotionally to deal with the difficult questions asked. They might not have ever even thought about the question. Be prepared to revisit the issues, ask questions differently, or give the victim time and space to answer the question. Repeat interviews may be necessary, especially for a victim that can only psychologically tolerate pieces at a time.

Especially in the case of intimate violence, it is of the utmost importance not to force the victim into making a prosecutorial decision before they are ready. Intimate partner violence is a very dynamic situation. The victim could be living with someone who is threatening them or promising that they will get counseling and change. A prosecutor who forces a victim into committing early on whether she will prosecute might be missing a big opportunity. The aim of these interviews is to communicate to the victims that the team believes them, does not judge them, and is willing to give them time to make an informed decision about their own lives.

A prosecutor who is patient but clear in terms of expectations and realities will be able to get rapport and trust from the victim than one who is rushed and pressures the victim for information or decisions. Initially, a victim may not want anything to do with you in the beginning stages of a case. The offender may have influenced her to see the prosecutor as an enemy. But if you demonstrate that you want to keep the lines of communication open, to be someone that will listen and not judge, you will be surprised by how many victims will come back when the tide turns at home, which it almost inevitably does.

Conducting an Effective Interview

An effective offender-focused interview is characterized by a victim who is comfortable giving the narrative, guided by a prosecutor who is actively listening and informative. An effective interviewer is patient, makes the speaker feel listened to, and knows the right questions and how to ask them. An effective interview does not have to last hours or strain the prosecutor's resources, but it needs to consist of interviewer skills and an understanding of the victim's issues.

Creating a Dialogue

A crucial part of creating and maintaining an effective interview is engaging in active listening without unnecessarily interrupting the victim's narrative. Active listening includes that the listeners interject comments to show they are listening. Active listeners encourage the victim to continue talking, asking for clarification, or supporting the victim through difficult questions, saying things like, "I know this is hard, I can wait while you think about it." While a good interviewer may jot notes or points to return to, it is challenging to document the victim's narrative and listen simultaneously. Make sure there is a competent note-taker present during your interview. This has a dual role. The interviewer does not have to take all the notes, which can result in not hearing the victim. More importantly, the interviewer does not risk becoming a witness. If you jot notes, just let the victim know they are for you, so you can return to the subject without interrupting what she is saying.

Further, a prosecutor should explain the questions being asked. There may be frequent turnover of prosecutors in intimate violence cases, sometimes these victims may have talked to multiple investigators and prosecutors. This can be extremely frustrating for the victim, who has to recall the assault repeatedly. A new prosecutor should simply explain to the victim that while the prosecutor is familiar with the case file, some questions will be redundant and that it is important to understand the facts from the victim's perspective, not through the translation of others. The prosecutor can remind the victim that it is essential to get it right, so there may be questions about the assault to ensure the appropriate charges. These questions are not about the credibility of the victim – reassure the victim that. This simple explanation goes a long way with victims because some truly believe that when they get asked the same questions repeatedly, the prosecutor does not believe them or is trying to "trip them up." A simple explanation of the questions can remove the victim's doubt and fear, going a long way toward building the crucial trust and confidence that will enable the victim to testify in the best way possible.

The Victim's Narrative

The victim's narrative is the most vital part of the investigation. Invite the victim to begin with her own words at her own pace. The prosecutor can facilitate the interview in a few different ways. Allow the victim to control the pace. Prompting the victim to go on or explain more or asking open-ended questions helps maintain the flow of information. Avoid leading or closed-ended questions, as having the victim only answer "yes" or "no" shifts the burden of the interview to the interviewer, who has to ask the right questions.

During the victim's narrative, tolerate silence. Do not be afraid of it. Silence can be awkward, but interviewers need to embrace it, especially when it comes to victim interviews. When a victim is silent after a question, there can be a natural tendency to fill the silence. This practice can have unintended consequences. For instance, when you ask a victim what stopped her from calling 911 and she pauses, if you fill the silence with the "answer" you think is correct ("you were scared" or "maybe you didn't think they would believe you"), you have just telegraphed the answer to the victim. In an unfamiliar situation, the victim will be looking to the interviewer for clues about what is "right" or acceptable. Whether true or not, the victim may agree with you, and you have lost the benefit of the true answer. When faced with silence, be patient. Do not force an answer. Give the victim time to think. If a response is not forthcoming, move on or offer the victim a break.

After the victim gives an initial narrative, the interviewer has the opportunity to go back and get clarification or ask unanswered questions. Sometimes victims speak quickly, only superficially discussing essential details. After the initial narrative, the prosecutor or interviewer should take the time to go back and ask specific questions. If the victim was disorganized chronologically, this is the time to begin to organize the narrative. Unless the interviewer has become completely confused, it is acceptable for the victim to start anywhere in time during the crime. The victims must begin the narrative where they feel comfortable. As a prosecutor, understanding the two days before the event may seem insignificant. But it could be imperative to the victim to explain choices and provide a context to the prosecutor so that she will be understood.

Before the interviewer ends the interview, always ask victims if there were things not asked that they expected or wanted to say. There are things that victims think are important that prosecutors do not. Conversely, there are things that prosecutors consider important that victims do not. For example, close to trial, one victim revealed that reporting to the police was not the first time she had told anyone about the assault. This author asked the victim who she had told after she called the police, to which she replied that she had told her mother, but it was before she called the police. The prosecutor on the case confronted the victim about why she had not said that prior. There were two obvious reasons. No one had asked her who she told. And the victim had no way of knowing that it was significant to know that she told her mother. What was natural for a victim, call her mother for help, was a previously unknown "excited utterance" for prosecutors. Another victim revealed to these authors before trial that the rapist had also put his finger in her vagina. The young woman did not tell about the finger because she believed that legally, only being penetrated by a penis was part of sexual assault. It took these learning experiences to realize how much information the victim has that the prosecutor may never know without the right questions.

The Interview Questions

In an offender-focused interview, the right questions involve gathering as much information for identifying evidence and the offender's behavior as possible. It is tempting in a complicated case to begin to focus on the victim, especially if that victim has engaged in behaviors that the prosecutor fears explaining to a jury.

There are many ways to ask a question. Some are directive. Some are clarifying. Some questions are blaming, communicating the message that there was a "right" thing that the victim did not do or say. To ask the right questions, the investigator and prosecutor must understand the broader context of intimate violence. The abuse exists outside the moment of the crime. The interviewer should gather information about the time before and after the assault and the relationship between the offender and victim. The interviewers must believe that most victim behavior can be explained with the right information and that most victims' responses make sense but exist in the context of abuse. Concentrating your questions on how the offender's behavior influenced the victim's choices will lead to an open dialogue that will later help you frame the assault. Additionally, properly asked questions will elicit sensory details that help corroborate the victim's version of the assault. There are many questions that can be asked if asked in a way so as not to blame or shame the victim.

Gathering facts is more manageable than questioning a victim about the victim's feelings, thoughts, or decision-making, especially if those choices seem confusing or counterintuitive. The victims will hide or deny information of which they are ashamed or embarrassed. The victims might try to appear ideal or believe they must be blameless to be worthy of justice. They might not even know what is problematic legally. The most difficult part of interviewing victims is asking questions that involve issues that could prompt the victim to defend herself, feel confused, or feel judged. Yet prosecutors must ask these questions to understand the victim and the potential challenges of the case.

Asking the Hard Questions

The hardest part of the victim interview is asking difficult questions about the victim's behaviors and history. The most difficult areas to broach are the "counterintuitive" responses of the victims – the behaviors or decisions that confound the juries and judges, leading to erroneous conclusions about events. Some prosecutors refer to these issues as "bad" facts of the case. Change the language around the issues first; these are *challenging* facts, not bad facts. They are challenging not because the victim did something "bad," but because the fact finders may have trouble understanding the victim's responses. The prosecutor cannot avoid these questions. In fact, presenting the challenging issues during the merits of the case deflates their impact of them during the defense's presentation.

Numerous issues continuously arise in crimes of intimate violence. Why did she stay in an abusive relationship? Why didn't she fight back? Why didn't she immediately report the crime? We have addressed some of the issues that impact victim response, but an offender-focused interview allows the prosecutor to concentrate on the offender's actions. Why are we focusing on the victim's responses when the victim is not the criminal in the case? Instead of asking why the victim did this or that, we should be asking about the offender's decisions and behaviors. The question is not "why did she stay," but "why does he abuse her?"

If prosecutors are offender-focused, they can learn how to craft questions that address the challenges while simultaneously focusing on the offender. It is often the actions of the offender that dictate the victim's choices. If you explore why the victim stayed, you may hear things such as "I thought he would change," "he told me he would take the kids away from me if I left," or "I just wanted back the man I married – I had hope." These answers make the victims' choices understandable. And they highlight the offenders' behaviors – manipulating, threatening, or apologizing. From that perspective, the victims' "counterintuitive" behaviors make more sense.

Constructing questions in the interview that get a victim to reflect provides powerful information. The victim can recreate the experience of the offender for the prosecutor and then, the fact finders. If prosecutors are not afraid of the challenging facts in the case and allow the victim to explain, there is a much higher chance for a successful prosecution. Do not avoid the issues. Do not hope the defense will not bring up acts that might be difficult to understand. Confront the challenging facts head-on and give the victim an opportunity to explain her decisions.

How to Ask the Difficult Questions

When asking questions regarding "counterintuitive" behavior, it seems the easiest thing to do is simply ask the victim "why?" Why didn't you call the police right away? Why did you go back to him? However expedient this question may be, it is a very detrimental question. The question "why" is very judgmental. If someone walked up to you on the street and asked why you were wearing the shirt you had on, you assume they thought there was something wrong with it. The question "why" implies that there is judgment, a condemnation, or a violation of an expectation. That is exactly how victims can feel when an interviewer asks why they made the choices they did. Asking why a victim did not resist intimates that she should have resisted. The question of why may echo the self-doubt or blame the victim is already feeling. Additionally, the question "why" rarely solicits a helpful answer. The answer to why is typically, "I don't know."

There are several ways of asking difficult questions without sounding judgmental and keeping the interview offender-focused. Remember the ways questions can start – what? When? How? Also, answers can be prompted by phrases like "tell me about," "help me understand," or describe. The interviewer can focus on the victims' internal experiences to solicit personal details that lend to a victim's credibility. Some examples include:

- What did you do to cope with that?
- What did you do next?
- What were you thinking during the assault?
- What were you feeling when he …?
- What made you decide not to scream?

- How did you keep yourself safe?
- What was going through your mind when ...?
- What kept you from (screaming, fighting, leaving)?

Asking these questions instead of why achieves two purposes. First, by avoiding a judgmental question, the victim will provide more insightful and informative responses because she is going through her thought process. "Why did you stay" will result in "I don't know," because there might not be a good enough answer for the victim. "What kept you from leaving" could elicit more thoughtful, sympathetic, and understandable responses, like "I loved him," "I didn't want to lose everything," "I thought he would kill me," or "I was afraid no one else would love me." Each of these responses can trigger another question, most often about something the offender did that affected the victim's choices. For instance, if you ask the victim what she was thinking when she texted the rapist back after he reached out to her, she might tell you she was afraid to alert him that something was wrong. With this simple question, she has explained her "counterintuitive" behavior AND shown that her choice to text him back was born out of her fear of retaliation. More of these offender-focused questions are available in Appendix A.

The other tricky area that must be covered in a substantive interview is negative information about the victim that needs to be verified. The most common example is a victim's previous sexual history. All states must protect victims under the Federal rape shield law, established by the Violence Against Women Act in 1994. This law attempts to protect a victim from undue scrutiny of her sexual history. However, states vary in the strength of this law. Whether the prosecutor's state has strong or weak laws, prosecutors owe it to victims to do their best to protect them from irrelevant and, quite frankly, harassing questions about their sexual history. But, a prosecutor cannot file a pre-emptive motion to exclude these questions unless the prosecutor has the information. This requires asking the victim about the relevant information. A prosecutor should not be asking victims about their sexual history as a matter of course. The information should be explored when there is information from a witness, a Sexual Assault Forensic Exam report when victims are asked about recent consensual sex, or the defense.

This can be daunting. Victims can become highly defensive, wondering why their sexual behavior is "any of your business." They can be upset, feeling violated or victimized by the process. To minimize the negative impact on the victim of these questions, approach the subject with sensitivity. Blame the defense for making her behavior an issue. For example, it can be useful to ask at the start of exploring the challenging information, "What is the worst thing that the offender told his team about you?" The victim might offer up some of the information you have already attained. Explain the importance or relevance of the questions. Preface your questions by indicating that it may not be true, but even if it is, it does not change what you believe about the case or your judgment of the victim. Explain the importance of honesty and completeness in the victim's responses, adding your ability to file motions to exclude irrelevant information. This same tactic needs to be used with other areas where the victim might need protection, like mental health history. Victims might want to volunteer their mental health history to show their trauma without realizing the humiliation and problems that can accompany that type of scrutiny and exposure.

Identifying All Charges and 404(b)

A vital goal of the substantive interview is to identify all potential charges and any other "bad acts" evidence that can help corroborate the victim's testimony. This is particularly important in crimes of intimate violence, where the victim often lives in an environment of abuse that shapes her behaviors. To create this environment for the fact finders, the prosecutor must be able to present behaviors of the offender that are not charged. In order to do that, the prosecutor must collect information from the victim outside the context of the charged assault.

Federally and in many states, this is referred to as 404(b) evidence.[1] Evidence of this nature is evidence of other crimes or "bad acts" that a prosecutor can introduce in the case in chief. This evidence cannot be introduced to prove propensity or predisposition but can be used to demonstrate motive, opportunity, preparation, knowledge, or intention, among other things. This is important in crimes of intimate violence to reveal the offender's understanding and motivation for the abusive behavior, psychological maltreatment, or other controlling behavior that serves to degrade, dominate, oppress, or control the victim. The preceding acts manipulate and dictate how the victim acts and thinks. These acts sustain the offender's domination and relationship with the victim. To truly convey the meaning and impact of the crime, as well as explain and clarify the victim's behaviors, it is vital for the prosecutor to understand and be prepared to present this information.

As previously described, the Power and Control wheel is an excellent tool to help guide the victim during the interviewer's collection of "bad acts" evidence. Also, reviewing the questions on a lethality assessment can reveal even more damaging information. While most of the offender's behavior may not be chargeable, referring to emotional and financial abuse, describing the abuse certainly presents a complete picture of the victim's daily life with the abuser. Most victims will not think to talk about emotional, psychological, or financial abuse; they don't consider it criminal. But when this information is available, the prosecutor can present the complete picture of what goes on within that household. The prosecutor can corroborate the victim's account and describe how the offender's actions affected the victim's choices.

Summary

Offender-focused interviewing is a powerful way of attaining information in a way that builds the most rapport and does the least harm to victims. The prosecutor gathers information that fleshes out the case against the offender, enabling the prosecutor to present a full portrait of the defendant who ultimately committed the chargeable crime. Additionally, it allows the prosecutor to support the victim without making the case about defending the victim. In conclusion:

- Offender-focused interviewing should be a goal for prosecutors dealing with intimate violence crimes.
- Offender-focused interviewing requires skill development, especially in terms of constructing questions that focus on the offender to illuminate the offender's influence over the victim.
- The prosecutor should not avoid challenging aspects of the case. Constructively worded questions can elicit information and support the victim even in the most difficult situations.
- It is critical to broaden the focus of cases of intimate violence to include acts outside the assault or charged incident.

Chapter 8

Pre-trial Strategy

Successful trials rely on the prosecutors' analysis and implementation of offender-focused pre-trial strategies. Several components include developing themes and theory, filing pre-trial motions, and deciding how to best use experts. Identifying issues in the case and getting rulings about them makes the actual trial more predictable. In addition, maximizing expert assistance pre-trial in developing themes, conducting victim and witness interviews, and providing testimony for pre-trial motions can further enhance and solidify the case before trial.

The Importance of Theme

Always remember – a trial without a theme is a trial without a purpose. Theme is often confused with theory. The theory is the legal basis for prosecution and why the prosecutor's version of the crime is compelling to the fact finder. A theme is different. The theme is the encapsulation of the theory of your case. It is the lens through which the jury views the evidence. An effective theme allows jurors to organize information, directing them to the prosecutor's arguments and evidence, making the theory easier to understand and remember.

A good theme is like a tagline in a movie or a commercial. The prosecutor's goal is to not just make the theme strong enough to carry A message, but YOUR message. One of the most famous themes of all time is from the O.J. Simpson trial – "if the glove don't fit, you must acquit." Decades later, it persists in people's memory, and still holds power. Unfortunately for the prosecution, it was the defense theme, but it was extremely effective.

Prosecutors sometimes forgo developing a theme, believing it is "corny" or seems contrived. Years of practice have taught me the importance of themes in terms of keeping not only the prosecution team but also the jury focused on the main issues in the case. In addition, the absence of a prosecution theme allows the defense to define the issues. The jury must rely on your theme to organize and characterize evidence and decide disputed facts.

Developing a Theme

An effective theme is short, easy to remember, and specifically tailored to the facts of the case. It must also be offender-focused. It must also accurately characterize the case without overly dramatic or over-promising the evidence. For example, a theme of "predator versus prey" is tempting in a sexual assault case. But if the case involves a young college student who happens upon an unconscious, intoxicated, or sleeping victim and sexually assaults her, the "predator versus prey" theme might be an over-reach for a jury that could expect much different testimony and evidence. If your theme is predator versus prey, the jury makes expect the defendant to be a

DOI: 10.4324/9781003121855-11

stranger that stalked and set a trap to assault the victim. When the jury hears the facts of a defendant "happening upon" the victim and that it was someone she knew, they may feel misled. Also, themes, like theories are not static. As the investigation unfolds and more evidence is uncovered, the theory may change, necessitating the theme changes as well.

There are many sources to look to find and develop a theme. The theme may come from the victim's statements, a witness statement, and especially, the offender's own words. Frequently, the offender's statement is replete with quotes that can serve as a theme. This is especially true if those quotes show arrogance, callousness, or disregard for the norms of society and/or the law. If choosing to use an offender's quote, do not forget the Rule of Completeness (F.R.E. 106). The Rule of Completeness is a rule of evidence that entitles an opposing party to introduce an entire statement if the other side introduces a partial statement. The prosecutor must be prepared for the entire statement to come in, not just the portions picked out as favorable.

Using and Maximizing Theme

Minimally, the prosecutor should begin and end with the case theme. The most effective use of theme occurs when it is woven throughout all aspects of the trial – from voir dire through closing and rebuttal. An effective theme is maximized to ensure that the jury takes that theme back to the deliberation room.

There are several ways to maximize your theme. They are based on the psychology of thinking and memory. When a theme is woven throughout the entire case, from voir dire to closing, the prosecutor utilizes the advantage of both *primacy* and *recency*. Jurors tend to develop their beliefs on the information they receive first (primacy) and tend to retain what they hear last (recency). It is why you want to begin and end your opening and closing with the same phrase. A powerful, simple phrase reiterated at the beginning and end of each opportunity to frame the case for the jury can maximize the theme's impact.

Another way to maximize the theme is through alliteration. Alliteration is a simple language tool where the words in the sentence begin with the same letter. Usually, it is most effective in threes because it is short and is easier to remember. An example is "He was Calculated, Callous and Cruel" as a theme to describe the intimate partner abuser who battered his partner for years.

A more advanced way to maximize the theme is anchoring. Anchoring is a word, phrase, or movement the prosecutor repeats throughout the case. Through repetition, certain aspects of your narrative or evidence are reinforced in the jury's minds. One of the best examples of anchoring is Martin Luther King's "I Have a Dream" speech. Dr. King repeats "I have a dream" at the beginning of eight paragraphs. He also uses the word "freedom" 20 times, "dream" 11 times, and "we" 30 times. His use of repetition helped convey inspiration and inclusivity, inviting the listeners. Anchoring invites the jury to follow the prosecutor's arguments and reasoning; because of the repetition, the jury knows when you will repeat your theme.

Thematic Reversal

Thematic reversal is a technique that can be very useful, but risky. Done poorly, it can be used by the defense against the prosecutor. Thematic reversal is adopting the defense theme to co-opt it for the prosecution. This most often occurs when the prosecutor thematically reverses the defense theme in rebuttal. The prosecutor did this effectively in a sexual assault trial witnessed by this author.

The defense's theme in closing was "Poor Choices." The defense listed all the things the victim did with the offender, drinking with him, getting a ride with him, and going back to his room, hoping to evoke victim-blaming and rape myths in the jury so they would nullify. In rebuttal, the prosecution stood up with a PowerPoint slide that simply said "Poor choices are not rape-able offenses." The prosecution went on to argue that every one of the victim's "poor choices" was directly attributable to the defendant. He furnished the alcohol and gained the victim's trust by promising to take her to a safe place to sleep for the night. This is most effective in rebuttal because the prosecutor has the last word. Again, take heed; the defense can also do it to the prosecution, so ensure that you are testing your theme with your co-workers, friends, and family.

Rules to Live By: Creating Offender-Focused Themes

There are several essential principles to developing and utilizing a theme. The prosecutor needs to be comfortable repeating it. The theme must focus on the offender's choices and actions. Themes should not suggest propensity. Prosecutors must also avoid trying to be too clever. If a theme seems too cutesy or over the top, it will come off as contrived and will likely be ignored, vitiating the entire point of having a theme in the first place. Therefore, it is imperative to test the theme on non-lawyers.

The theme should be evocative, communicating the evidence accurately, setting the stage for the case. Especially in cases of intimate violence, themes can be personal, telegraphing some of the victims' experience and the offenders' malice. Again, the prosecutor can effectively capture the experience and trauma of an intimate crime without being overly dramatic or over-promising the case. Examples of offender-focused themes include:

- He Made Her Bedroom His Crime Scene.
- The One She Least Suspected Became the One She Had to Fear Most.
- He Was a Stranger That Night.
- "As I lost consciousness, I prayed that my kids knew how much I loved them."
- "When she cried, it made me want to rape her more."
- He Went From the Best of Bosses to the Most Brutal Betrayer.
- Bloodied, Battered, and Bruised.

Pre-trial Motions

Besides the effective use of theme, pre-trial motions, or motions in limine, are another strategy that can focus the prosecution on the offender and attempt to protect the victim. Two of the most important of these are rape shield motions and mental health privilege motions. Additionally, prosecutors can file motions in limine to prevent the defense from presenting information that is more prejudicial than probative (F.R.E. 403) or would cause undue embarrassment or harassment of a witness (F.R.E. 611).

Rape Shield Motions

Rape shield motions protect victims from degrading, embarrassing disclosures of intimate details of their private sexual lives. These motions can become complicated, balanced with preserving a defendant's constitutional right to present a defense. As discussed, a prosecutor must be thoroughly familiar with their jurisdiction's rape shield statutes.

For continuity purposes, we will refer to the Rape Shield Law found in section 412 of the Federal Rules of Evidence. Rule 412 applies to any proceeding that involves an alleged sex offense. It is designed to prevent evidence that the victim engaged in *other sexual behavior or to show a victim's sexual predisposition*. Sexual behavior, by this definition, includes any sexual behavior not encompassed by the alleged offense. Sexual predisposition refers to a victim's mode of dress, speech, or lifestyle that does not directly refer to sexual activities or thoughts but that may have a sexual connotation for the factfinder. F.R.E. 412 can be obtained here: https://www.govinfo.gov/content/pkg/USCODE-2015-title28/pdf/USCODE-2015-title28-app-federalru-dup2-rule412.pdf. Rule 412 – The Victim's Sexual Behavior or Predisposition says:

(a) **Prohibited Uses.** The following evidence is not admissible in a civil or criminal proceeding involving alleged sexual misconduct:
   (1) evidence offered to prove that a victim engaged in other sexual behavior; or
   (2) evidence offered to prove a victim's sexual predisposition.
(b) **Exceptions.**
   (3) *Criminal Cases.* The court may admit the following evidence in a criminal case:
      (A) evidence of specific instances of a victim's sexual behavior, if offered to prove that someone other than the defendant was the source of semen, injury, or other physical evidence;
      (B) evidence of specific instances of a victim's sexual behavior with respect to the person accused of the sexual misconduct, if offered by the defendant to prove consent or if offered by the prosecutor; and
      (C) evidence whose exclusion would violate the defendant's constitutional rights.

The exceptions under 412 (b)(1)(A) and (B) are self-explanatory. However, prosecutors must guard against the exception under (C). This last exception, otherwise known as the constitutional exception, allows the defense to argue that it is constitutionally required for the defendant. Yet, it is possible or probable that what the defense is really attempting to do is reveal the victim's sexual predisposition, to humiliate, intimidate, or embarrass her while tainting the jury against her, commonly referred to as "slut shaming." Commonly, the defense may argue that the victim's sexual activity with someone else is tied to the victim's motive to lie. For instance, she is married, and the sex with the defendant was consensual, but the victim is "crying rape" because she is trying to protect her marriage. Another example is that the sex with the defendant was consensual, but the victim claimed it was sexual assault because he did not want anyone to know he is gay.

Protecting Mental Health Records: Therapist-Client Privilege

Most states have enacted laws addressing the subjects of confidentiality and privileged communication between clients and therapists/counselors. Most statutes described the therapist/counselor-client privilege as "same as attorney-client privilege," whereas other statutes refer to the State's rules of evidence. Prosecutors need to be familiar with their relevant statutes. While most states provide for confidentiality between counselors and clients, there are exceptions to client confidentiality or privilege. Standard exceptions include the following:

1 When the mental health provider is formally reporting to or consulting with administrative supervisors, colleagues, or supervisors who share professional responsibility and are also bound by privilege;
2 When the client gives written consent to share information;

3 When the client reveals the intent to commit an act that presents a clear, imminent risk of serious mental or physical harm or injury to another, or is a serious threat to public safety and the provider is bound to warn or forestall the threat;
4 When the client waives the privilege by bringing any public charges against the licensee; and,
5 When the client reveals information involving abuse or suspected abuse of a minor.

Being the victim of a crime does not waive the victim's privilege. However, the defense will generally request the victim's mental health history and/or records in their discovery request. They may argue that a mental health diagnosis is related to the fabrication of allegations. The defendant may be seeking corroboration of his claims that the victim is bipolar or has "conflated" memories of others who have abused her. While even the victims themselves may not "fear" the disclosure of their mental health histories or have a prior disclosure in their therapy, the prosecutor should try to protect the victims' privacy and privilege. There can be many unforeseen consequences to exposing the victims to the scrutiny of their mental health records, especially because the victims typically have no accurate idea of what has been documented, which may be inaccurate, subject to the provider's interpretation, or incomplete.

The prosecutor should not participate in trying to obtain the victim's mental health records. The best practice is to deny that request as neither relevant nor necessary, forcing the defense to file a motion to compel. The prosecution should show the victim a willingness to fight the defense request and, unless ordered by the judge, should not facilitate the procurement of records. Often, these requests are a defense tactic to scare the victim into not participating out of fear that her private thoughts and possible diagnoses will not only be exposed but also specifically shared with the person who has abused her.

If, for some reason, the judge appears inclined to order disclosure of the records, there are still steps that the prosecutor can take to lessen the impact on the victim. First, request that the court do an in-camera review to determine what, if anything, is relevant. The prosecution should request that only the portions of the records that the judge finds relevant be turned over to the defense. In addition, the prosecution should ask for the records to be sealed and returned by the defense, to the court or prosecution after the trial so they are not available to the defendant to use nefariously later.

Other Relevant Motions

Other relevant motions in limine can be filed, including motions to pre-admit evidence and motions to exclude irrelevant issues and/or are designed to harass or humiliate the victim. Motions to pre-admit evidence may include hearsay statements and other bad acts known as F.R.E. 404(b), discussed in a previous chapter. Prosecutors should seek rulings on these relevant issues as to whether certain statements or events may be introduced as these decisions impact the case. If the information must be introduced through a victim's or witness' testimony, the directs must be crafted appropriately to allow the prosecutor to prep the victim and witnesses.

Rulings in these pre-trial matters may determine whether the prosecution can even move forward on a particular charge. In interpersonal violence cases, victims commonly decide just before trial that they do not want to participate. Unless prosecutors know whether an excited utterance or statement for purposes of medical treatment and diagnosis will be admitted, they probably will not be able to go forward on the charge(s) that those statements support.

Similarly, knowing whether the judge will allow the prosecution to put on evidence of other bad acts will impact the direct examination and order of witnesses. Remember, if the judge denies the motion for 404(b) testimony in the prosecution's case in chief, it does not mean that testimony is completely foreclosed. The defense often opens the door to the testimony of other bad through the cross-examination of the victim or the direct of the defendant or other defense witnesses. Regardless of the judge's original ruling, the prosecutor should proceed as if the other bad acts testimony will become relevant. This will necessitate placing the other bad acts witnesses on their witness list and subpoena them for trial.

The Use of Expert Consultants

Another way to shape the battlefield of the trial is to utilize experts as consultants, regardless of whether the experts will testify. Medical experts and forensic psychologists/psychiatrists are two types of experts commonly used in cases of intimate violence. Both types of experts can help develop voir dire questions, clarify the opening and closing arguments, assist with interviews of victims and witnesses, and assist with the interview of the defense expert. Medical experts can help explain what the medical records mean and what they think is significant. It can be a surprise to prosecutors who can learn from the expert that what seemed to be an important medical finding was not, or, on the other hand, something that the prosecutor dismissed was significant. Experts can assist in helping shape and prep a treating clinician's testimony. Most treating clinicians have never testified before. Although they possess medical knowledge, they may need to learn how to best present that knowledge to a factfinder. The consulting expert can ensure that the clinician's direct testimony is precise, to the point, and not laden with jargon. The consultant can also be incredibly helpful in preparing the clinician for cross-examination.

A forensic psychologist or psychiatrist with experience with intimate violence victims can be useful in various ways. They can help prepare a victim for testimony, and help a victim explain what a fact finder may see as "counter-intuitive behavior." The expert can provide a more nuanced approach to asking questions, eliciting more detailed or different information that can be useful in testimony. The expert can assist the prosecutor in crafting questions to elicit the information or advise the prosecutor on how to interact with a traumatized victim. Sometimes, the prosecutor must be taught how to cope with the victims' extreme emotions or defense mechanisms, like shutting down on the stand. Forensic experts can also be incredibly helpful in developing the cross of the defendant. Their unique insight into how offenders think may help develop chapters for cross that the prosecutor can translate into appropriate cross-examination questions.

Summary

Trials can be time-consuming, arduous, and exhausting. The more issues the prosecutor can resolve or prevent pre-trial, the easier the actual trial may become. Organizing the case around a strong offender-focused theme, filing pre-trial motions, and utilizing experts at every stage of trial preparation are all valuable ways to minimize and mitigate the challenges and hurdles at trial. Shaping the trial plan before beginning voir dire can significantly reduce the risk of surprise and show the victim that you are willing to put the time and effort in to ensure you are doing your best to protect her. In conclusion:

- Developing an appropriate and accurate theme is highly valuable and gives the trial a direction and purpose attainable to the jury.
- There are strategies for developing and maximizing the theme to help ensure that the jury takes the theme into the deliberation room.
- Offender-focused themes cement the case in the actions and decisions of the perpetrator.
- Pre-trial motions can prevent surprises during the trial. Their rulings can help shape the direct examinations and order of witnesses.
- A prosecutor's preparation pre-trial should be aimed at exposing the offender, protecting the victim, and using resources, like consultants, as thoroughly as possible, increasing the probability of a successful trial.

Chapter 9

Selecting the Right Jury

Jury selection in crimes of intimate violence requires particular thoughtfulness and attention. As we have discussed previously, juries continue to maintain misinformation about intimate violence, as well as victims and offenders. Juries engage in biased thinking and victim-blaming. In offender-focused prosecution, addressing these issues in the jury is imperative, as is assessing the arenas that the prosecutor must address during the trial. Jury bias can impact a prosecutor's case in findings and sentencing, making jury selection a task of particular importance.

Goals of Voir Dire

Voir dire constitutes a critical part of a jury trial for both the defense and the jury. Although the desired outcome of a jury trial differs between the prosecution and the defense, both sides have similar goals in selecting a jury. A juror must be fair and impartial, affording both sides the opportunity for an unbiased analysis of the case. Effective voir dire can accurately identify jurors and ferret out juror biases about the victim, the offender, or the criminal justice system. According to the Judicial Education Center (http://jec.unm.edu/education/online-training/stalking-tutorial/voir-dire-and-jury-selection), the goals for effective voir dire include:

- Gathering information about individual prospective jurors regarding their potential to be fair-minded and impartial,
- Assessing the jurors' ability to apply the law as instructed;
- Educating the jury about the parties' respective theories of the case;
- Developing rapport with and earning the trust and respect of the jury;
- Making the jury see the prosecutors as trustworthy, dedicated, and hardworking professionals;
- Ensuring the jury considers the victim as deserving of justice for all that the victim has experienced;
- For the prosecution, making sure the accused stays solidly identified as the offender;
- Introducing the jury to potential problem areas in the case to begin managing those weaknesses; and
- Demystifying the jury trial process to emphasize the importance, power, and serious nature of jury service in a society governed by the rule of law.

Meeting all these goals in an offender-focused prosecution requires the prosecutor to construct a comprehensive voir dire that addresses not only the case itself but also the jurors' pre-existing biases and myth acceptance.

DOI: 10.4324/9781003121855-12

The Three Pillars of Voir Dire

The three pillars of voir dire are having thematic questions, eliminating bias, and rehabilitating favorable members. In cases of intimate violence, the prosecutor must imbue all the voir dire with an offender-focus, from identifying and eliminating bias to rehabilitating jurors who are willing to be or are educated about the issues in intimate violence.

First, you must recognize what issues are in your case that might elicit bias or reliance on misinformation in the jurors. The areas might require the education of the jurors during the case or the confrontation and mitigation of bias. These issues can range from everyday societal issues to explaining counter-intuitive behaviors. The relevant societal issues could include race, sexuality, religion, gender stereotypes, and myths about intimate violence. The prosecutor must prepare to address the issues that made the team cringe when they were revealed, recognizing that if the team is questioning some of the facts or the victim's behaviors, the jury will too.

It is imperative to assess potential jurors for their willingness to be educated or whether their biases are too deeply ingrained to allow them to serve. Once the issues are identified, the prosecutor can decide how to address them through thematic questions (teaching) or eliminating bias (hunting).

Thematic Questions

The best voir dire comes from a thorough case analysis. In offender-focused prosecution, that case analysis has identified the numerous issues that may confuse the jury or be used to misdirect the jury, causing them to adhere to myths and misinformation. Voir dire questions in offender-focused cases have themes that address the misconceptions of intimate violence and remind a jury about points they may forget when struck by the seriousness of the crime. For instance, juries may simply forget that most crime is without witness when they are told that a sexual assault is "he said, she said," and that there were no witnesses.

Theme-based questions introduce concepts specific to the case and prepare the jurors to hear those concepts addressed repeatedly. Through these questions, a prosecutor can commit potential jurors to ideas, then remind them throughout the case that they agreed to be open to accepting the idea. Thematic questions are designed to present and familiarize the jurors with a matter in the case, not to identify challenges. Introducing a factor of the case in the beginning and getting the juror to anticipate information regarding the factor can circumvent efforts to exploit the issue during trial. For example, a common issue in intimate partner violence involves the victim's lack of resistance or failure to call the police. Voir dire questions that address these issues might include:

- Is there anyone who expects the victim to at least scream or yell for help?
- Is there anyone here who could not convict the defendant if the victim did not resist the assault?
- Would you agree that in a robbery case if an offender demanded your wallet that the advice from law enforcement would be to just give it to the offender and not risk harm?
- Can anyone think of a reason why a victim may not want to call the police right away?
- Is there anyone here who would not be able to convict the defendant if the victim did not report the assault to the police immediately?
- Are you all willing to at least listen to the reasons the victim did not report to the police right away?

Then in closing, the prosecutor can remind the jury about what they agreed to in voir dire. The closing could include something like this:

> *Think back to the defense's cross of Mrs. Jones. She didn't resist him. She didn't cry out to the children for help. She didn't even call the police. Each of you agreed in voir dire that a victim does not have to resist, does not have to scream out. You also agreed to listen to the victim's reason for not calling the police immediately. And she told you why. She told you she did not want police in the house dragging him out of the house in handcuffs in front of the children.*

Because the prosecutor in voir dire introduced the issues and asked for the jurors' commitment to consider that the victim's response was reasonable, the prosecutor has a pre-established touch-point to return to with the jury. The prosecutor can remind the jury that they agreed to take the victim's explanation into account, eschewing their biases.

Identifying and Eliminating Bias

Sometimes, a juror will identify a bias or reveal a belief or experience that requires them to be challenged as a juror. Voir dire questions that address biases and victim blaming, as well as issues that eliminate offender accountability, are helpful to force out biases. Questions that address victim-blaming, excuses for violence, alcohol's mitigating impact on responsibility, gender roles, or minimization of intimate violence are useful in identifying juror biases that can be detrimental to the case. Examples might include questions about whether a victim deserved the assault, how the victim assumed the risk (what did she think was going to happen?), if the victim allowed the abuse (because she went back), or if the offender is not to blame for his reaction. Beliefs about anger leading to violence, alcohol being the cause of violence, or provocation sexually or physically being a reason for abuse are all jury biases that can be exploited in these cases. Additionally, jurors may still believe that intimate violence is a family problem, not a crime, or that someone cannot rape his spouse. These are the issues that must be identified.

If the prosecutor knows that the juror's bias or belief is harmful to impartiality in the case, the prosecutor must be prepared to challenge for cause. For instance, if a person says, notwithstanding the law, she would be unable to convict with just the victim's testimony, the prosecutor must adopt this (however painful that may be). If the prosecutor is confident that the juror's stance is undesirable, the prosecutor can seek affirmation of the juror's position with comments or questions that support a challenge. For example, saying, "it seems like you've given some thought to that" allows the juror to confirm the commitment to the positions. Highlighting the juror's struggle with disavowing a belief or bias is also effective. Questions like, "Even if the judge tells you that is not the law it would be hard for you to set that thinking aside, right?" or "So that is not a concept you can just compartmentalize or forget, is it?" can be very useful. This allows the juror to affirm the stance justified by the perceived support for the opinion. Making the juror's position seem understandable can embolden them to be forthright about it.

Rehabilitating a Juror

If the prosecutor finds a juror that answers favorably to the case without revealing issues that can trigger a defense challenge, the prosecutor can move on to the next juror. However, if the potential juror has said anything that the defense may try to characterize as an issue for a challenge, follow up with questions that demonstrate the potential juror is not biased. Questions such as, "Regardless how you feel about X, you agree to impartially decide whether the defendant is guilty or not guilty solely based on the evidence presented?" or "Notwithstanding X, you will follow the law and the Judge's instructions, right?" When a prosecutor has identified a potentially favorable or at least open juror, rehabilitating that juror with the appropriate questions is important.

Weaving the Theme through Voir Dire

As discussed in the previous chapter, the prosecutor must introduce the theme of the case in voir dire. Introducing the theme to the jury as soon as possible provides an initial framework that helps the jury organize information within the theme. At the very least, some voir dire questions should include and further the theme. Think about the critical element or elements of the theme. Is it power? Abuse of love? Violation of vows? The exploitation of status? A theme for a sexually abusive doctor may be "do no harm." Voir dire questions could address the jurors' expectation of professionalism and safety when seeking medical help.

To illustrate the process, consider a case involving the offender's exploitation of power over the victim. In the military, this might be the offender's superior rank over the victim. The theme could be "His weapon of choice was rank." Voir dire questions that further that theme are:

- Would you agree that some people abuse their rank (position)?
- Would you agree that a private might feel intimidated by a senior officer (or that an employee might feel intimidated by their boss)?
- Would you all agree that a significant difference in rank (position) could lead a person to believe that resisting an assault would be futile?
- Would you agree that a person may not report an assault if the person that assaulted them outranked them (as their boss) and they feared no one would believe them (they would be retaliated against, they would lose their job)?

From those questions, what does the jury already know about the case? There is a difference between the offender's and victim's in rank/position that the offender exploited. The victim did not resist, fearing negative consequences. And possibly that the victim did not report immediately. The questions are clearly offender-focused, pointing to the offender who influenced the decisions of the victim. The prosecutor begins to sow these seeds in voir dire and then reminds the jury in closing:

> *Private Jones never had a chance, nor was she even given one. The defendant used a weapon that is more effective than any gun or knife. He used his rank. He made it clear that her saying no would not matter to him because he held all the cards. He controlled her movements, her job, and, ultimately, her. Physical resistance wasn't an option; telling anyone was even less of an option. After all, as he told her that very night 'no one will ever believe you.' And when she finally got the courage, the command proved him right….*

Summary

Effective jury selection is directly related to case outcomes. Voir dire is the inauguration of the prosecutor's offender-focused case. It is a powerful means to embed the case's theme, ferret out biases and prejudice, and open the jurors' minds to education and reconsideration of the complex issue of intimate violence. In conclusion:

- Voir dire can be used to introduce the offender-focused theme through targeted questions.
- Although voir dire can be used to educate a jury, it is unlikely prosecutors will be able to change long-standing prejudices of jurors who believe intimate violence stereotypes and myths.
- Prosecutors will generally be more successful by eliminating jurors who hold such deep-rooted beliefs by asking questions that expose these beliefs.
- Prosecutors can set the stage for a successful prosecution by using questions at the start that further an offender-focused them.

Chapter 10

Trial

As prosecutors understand, intimate violence cases are complex, subtle, and ever-changing. The cases may go forward with a cooperating victim, only to lose that victim part way through. The evidence that unfolds can be dynamic, changing, and accumulating over the life of the trial. It can become challenging to remain offender-focused during the trial. In this chapter, you will find practical information for every stage of your trial, from opening to rebuttal.

Offender-Focused Opening (or How to Win the Case before You Present Evidence)

The art of a powerful opening statement involves clearly and logically presenting the theory of your case while anchoring your offender-focused theme in the jury's minds. As previously discussed, a good theme is crucial – not corny. By remembering the concepts of primacy and recency, prosecutors can structure the opening to encompass and reiterate the theme of the case, the vehicle that carries the theory. While the offender's motive is never required in a criminal case, it is always relevant. Juries want to know "why;" the prosecutor can be the first to tell them.

Often the offender's motive can become the theme. In crimes of intimate violence, anger, control, and revenge are all relevant motives transforming into effective themes. The theme or attention-getter should be the first thing the jury hears. The jury is anxiously awaiting information about what the case involves. They can be captured immediately by a quote from the victim, such as, "Please. Stop. I said no." This could be immediately followed by the theme of "He Never Cared What She Said, Only What He Wanted." Now the prosecutor has the jury's attention. Never begin an opening by thanking the jury; they want information. Thanking them can seem contrived and insincere, especially when they did not have a choice to be there. Let the jury know they are there for a good reason.

After getting the jury's attention with the theme or powerful statement or evidence, the prosecutor will explain the theory of the case in a narrative that brings the crime to life. Take the jury through the crime and the evidence in an active, assertive manner. The prosecutor is not telling a "story" or version; the prosecutor is telling the jury what happened. The opening is the prosecutor's first chance to present the case in the light they have chosen. Do not use the opening to "chase" the defense, defend the victim or try to thwart the defense story. The prosecutor can present some of the challenges or questions in the case but should not use the opening to focus on the defense's theory.

It is important to remember that less is more in the opening. The prosecutor should not fill a powerful opening with unimportant details. The prosecutor should want to avoid overwhelming the jury with times, dates, and names. Giving the most compelling issues in the case,

DOI: 10.4324/9781003121855-13

presenting the most striking elements of the crime is most impactful while not overselling the case. The prosecutor should never overpromise the evidence or discuss evidence that may not come out in trial. For example, you might not mention the DNA in the opening. And, given the changing nature of trials, a prosecutor should never promise what experts or other more peripheral witnesses will say. If the trial goes as many do, evidence and testimony may change. If things go well on direct of some witnesses, other witnesses, including experts, may become less relevant.

The opening should include some visuals. Most people (even judges) like to see things in addition to hearing things. It should not overwhelm the prosecutor's compelling recitation of the facts. Still, a well-placed picture of the scene, the victim's injuries, a timeline, or a PowerPoint with a relevant quote can be powerful. The prosecutor should present evidence in opening cautiously, though. Do not use evidence or quotes that may not come out in testimony. Only use what you can be sure will be presented in the trial. If it does not come out in trial, the defense will remind the jury in closing what the prosecutor promised in the opening was not delivered.

The most effective opening weaves the theme throughout the opening. At the very least, the opening should begin and end with what the prosecutor wants the jury to remember throughout the trial – *your* theme. A good practice with opening is to present it to others not involved in the case to ensure it does not overpromise the theory. Objective listeners can also tell if the defense could thematically reverse the theme in their opening or closing. The prosecutor's primary goal in the opening is to keep the focus on the offender. He is the reason you are in court. Convey the belief that nothing the victim did or said contributed to or caused the crime committed against her. By keeping the jury focused on the offender from the beginning, the prosecutor sends the message that the only person responsible for the crime they are considering is the offender, NOT the victim.

Offender-Focused Direct of the Victim (Why Not Ask Why, Redux)

A well-done direct should feel like an interesting conversation. Nothing derails an interesting conversation like someone (in this case, the witness) dominating it. Victims of violence can sometimes take over the direct. They are full of information that is meaningful to them but potentially problematic in court. Trauma can make them disorganized or derail them. It is important that the prosecutor provide a structure to the direct, without losing control of a witness who may be anxious, fearful, or responding to the offender in the room. Use "open" questions to allow a longer response from the victim. Then use "closed" or directive questions to shorten responses. For example, an "open" question may be, "Please describe the first time the accused hit you." The "closed" questions can be used on the follow-up to ensure specific information gets out and the elements get met. Some examples are, "Where were you when he first approached you?" or "What part of his body contacted what part of your body?" The prosecutor must be flexible and think quickly. You should be able to identify what the victim left out that you need or what you want to reiterate to the jury. It is important to listen to what the victim says instead of being wedded to a list of questions that suddenly do not make sense.

A good direct has specific transition statements that direct the witness to the subject the prosecutor wants to address. Remember that the victim may be overwhelmed with memories or not remember what the prosecutor wishes to elicit. Transition statements guide and structure the victim, often easing the victim's anxiety. Here is an example:

Q: Ms. Jones, I want to talk to you about Superbowl Sunday, 2020?

A: The first day he hit me?

Q: Where were you about 2 p.m. the day after he hit you?

A: I was in the hospital on Fort Belvoir, VA.

Use transition statements as often as you need. Do not let the victim flounder or guess. Directing the narrative minimizes the chance that the witness will say something objectionable or become flustered and upset. This might be the most challenging day of the witness' life. Everyone will appreciate the time saved. Also, when the prosecutor guides the direct, the counsel is in charge.

Another essential tool to use in a direct examination is looping. Looping is the technique of reiterating parts of the offense to connect a sequence and highlight important facts. The simplest form of looping is to make a vital answer part of the next question. For example:

Q: What did the accused do next?

A: He came over to the counter and grabbed the knife?

Q: When he grabbed the knife, what was going through your mind?

A: I was afraid he was going to kill me.

The victim's testimony forms the backbone of the case. Every other witness assists in the corroboration of her testimony or disabuses defense theories. The tone of the trial is set by the way the prosecutor develops the direct. Do not always assume the victim must testify first. While it makes sense chronologically because the victim knows the most about the crime, consider whether some witnesses can set the scene and have little to no impeachment on cross. These witnesses could include the first responding officers to describe the scene or a neighbor who heard the commotion. Also, consider putting some, if not all, allowable 404(b) evidence earlier in the case. This reveals and frames the defendant's plans, motives, and history, a foundation the prosecutor can build upon throughout the rest of the evidence.

Again, how the question is asked in direct is elemental to an effective offender-focused case and effective direct of the victim. Make sure the question is not blaming or judgmental. Ask questions so you do not convey doubts or skepticism to the jury. Do not ask the victim "why" unless it is purposeful and intentional. Structure the questions to focus on the offender.

An expert might be helpful in the construction of the prosecutor's direct. An expert can help guide the rapport between the prosecutor and the victim. Often, traumatized victims may remember things differently than time and date. For instance, a victim might recall an event by the house it occurred in, the season of the year, or the grade one of the children was in at the time. Listening to how a victim recalls information can help form an effective direct. In addition, if the victim struggles with trauma during the direct, a prosecutor can learn how to identify when a victim is struggling and how to help her. Too many prosecutors have had the experience of the victim "shutting down" on the stand and circumventing the testimony.

Constructing and Organizing the Direct

When developing the direct of the victim, keep the questions clear and focused. Good facts are more important than fancy questions. The prosecutor can accomplish this if you construct the direct by using chapters. Chapters are simply different topics that need to be covered. They can be short or long, with sub-chapters if it helps with organization. Build chapters with material, affirmative statements of fact that further the theory. In addition, predict the direction of the victim's cross and address the facts supporting the accused's theory. Appendix C offers examples of chapters.

Introducing the Victim to the Jury

The direct should begin by properly introducing and humanizing the victim. The judge and/or jury is charged with deciding the credibility of each witness – especially the victim. The prosecutor must elicit facts that show her education, background, job, hobbies, etc. so the factfinder sees the victim as an actual person and not the lying, vindictive person the defense will inevitably try to make her seem. Although there is no need to go through the victim's entire history, giving the jury a sense of her goals, mission, and achievements is important. Having the victim describe her personality or how she deals with conflict, her religion, or her culture can establish the foundation to explain her behaviors and responses to intimate violence. For example, if she was raised as a strict Catholic who was taught that divorce was not an option, staying in an abusive marriage makes sense.

There will be a limit to the questions allowed when trying to humanize the victim based on a relevance objection by the defense. The prosecutorial response to the objection is that the jury is the sole arbiter of credibility. They must understand the victim to understand her choices, which may seem "counter-intuitive" to them. Even if the judge stops you from asking these questions, do not simply discard the rest. Move them to the redirect chapters as they will inevitably become relevant once the victim is crossed on "why" she reacted in certain ways. Bringing out the victim's background, education, or personality later can explain why she did or did not do certain things, giving the jury an accurate lens to understand the victim's reactions. For instance, if the defense crosses the victim on why she stayed in the abusive relationship, the fact that she had a limited ability to work and no support system becomes very relevant as to why she *could* not leave the relationship.

Addressing the Challenging Facts

The next essential goal in direct is to identify and present any "challenging" facts. In this book, calling these facts "challenging" is intentional. Prosecutors often refer to facts that complicate their cases as "bad facts." These "bad" facts are usually something the victim did or did not do. By calling the issues "bad" facts, there is an inference that somehow the victim did something wrong. Do not seek to hide, "whitewash," or in any way bury challenging facts. Instead, seek to **identify** and **explain** them to the factfinders so that the factfinders can understand them. Almost all facts, when properly understood, can benefit the prosecutor's theme and theory of the case. The victim cannot effectively explain her choices unless the prosecutors allow the victim to do so ON DIRECT EXAMINATION.

One of the country's best and most respected former prosecutors is Mr. Vince Bugliosi. He has tried many high-profile cases, most notably the cases involving the murders perpetrated by Charles Manson and his "family." In his book about O. J. Simpson's acquittal (1996), Mr. Bugliosi addresses the prosecution's failure to confront the challenges of the case. He writes, "Another very surprising and harmful error the prosecution made in this case is that they frequently violated a basic, fundamental prosecutorial technique, namely, that when you know, the defense is going to present evidence damaging or unfavorable to your side, you present that evidence yourself (p. 86)." He laments that prosecutors allow damaging information to be introduced by the defense, not only because it allows the defense to control the information but also because the prosecutor has missed two valuable opportunities. Mr. Bugliosi goes on to explain (p. 86):

> Number one, it conveys to the jurors your willingness to see that all evidence, unfavorable to your case as well as favorable, comes out – that you are not trying to suppress it in open court or outside their presence. And this helps to establish your credibility with the jury. Secondly, it frequently converts a left hook by your opposition into a left jab. If it doesn't do that, it will almost always shave a few decibels from your opponent's trumpets. It indicates to the jury that the evidence can't really be all that bad if it was matter-of-factly and almost cavalierly brought out by you on direct exam of your own witness.

Mr. Bugliosi captures succinctly why a prosecutor would want to be the first to familiarize the jury with the challenging facts. It simply takes the impact out of these facts. They are already known and explained when the defense attempts to spring them on the victim. The victim can deflate the accusations or confrontation with these facts when they have been previously addressed and explained. Most importantly, the prosecutor and victim have already explored these "worst" facts; the victim is confident on the stand and those facts are not that bad because the prosecutor has not hidden them.

The prosecutor has to be extremely cognizant of how they ask the question when the direct exam questions address the challenging issues. We have discussed at length why not ask why in victim interviews. This instruction extends to the direct exam. Even if you have built a strong rapport with the victim and she knows you are not judging her by asking the "why" questions, there are up to thirteen people (the jury and the judge) remaining in that courtroom that may think you are judging the victim by asking the "why" questions. For instance, let's say the victim slept in the same bed as the offender after the sexual assault. The prosecutor should never make the victim deal with that fact for the first time on cross-examination, where she will likely be asked about it in a yes or no format. The direct examination should be used to provide a chance for the victim to explain her choices fully. It can proceed as follows:

Q: *Ms. Jones how did you physically feel once the sexual assault ended?*

A: I was so tired and confused. He was supposed to be a friend.

Q: *What prevented you from leaving his house after the assault?*

A: I was afraid of what he would do.

Q: *What made you afraid?*

A: He had his hands around my neck earlier. I didn't want him to think I was upset or angry so I figured I would pretend everything was ok.

Q: *Did you fall asleep in the bed?*

A: I did. I was exhausted.

Q: When did you feel safe to leave?

A: When I heard him snoring. I knew he was out cold so I grabbed what I could find and ran out of the house.

Q: You said you grabbed what you could. What did you leave behind?

A: My shoes, underwear, bra, and wallet. I could only find my yoga pants, shirt, phone, and keys.

Through the right questions, the prosecutor allows the victim to explain what seems to be an insurmountable fact into an easily understood explanation of the victim's circumstances and the emotions she was experiencing during the assault. The questions you ask must demonstrate the assault and its aftermath from the physical and emotional perspective of the victim. Sensory details are key. Ask what the victim heard, saw, smelled, tasted, and felt until you can picture it yourself. The sensory or emotional details are golden nuggets because the truth is in the details, building the victim's credibility until the jury realizes that the assault is not a fabrication. These questions encourage the jury to experience the assault through the victim's senses; they should see, hear, and feel the reality of the assault.

Best Practices for the Victim's Direct

First and foremost, prepare the direct early. It will undoubtedly change as more trial preparation is completed, but it is important to have at least an outline, some chapters, and a chronology to start. You should always be considering how to organize the direct-to-end on a powerful, emotional note. This is a fluid process because anyone who has specialized in intimate violence cases knows that you can discover new information up to the day before trial. Send your draft direct to a trusted someone who knows the basic facts, like a paralegal. Do not send it to someone who may be a potential witness (such as your forensic psychologist) because that makes the draft discoverable. This does not mean you cannot discuss the content of specific chapters or how to ask a question properly – this is exactly why we hire consultants. It just cannot be sent in writing to any potential witness.

You must prepare your victim but be wary of over-prepping. The victim's testimony is never going to be perfect. You cannot fix it by going over her testimony until she gets it "right." What over-prepping will accomplish is sowing mistrust between the prosecutor and the victim, making the victim feel pressured to memorize a script, and possibly making the victim seem insincere testifying because she is trying so hard to get it "right," she is not testifying from a place of trust and emotion. If possible, avoid prep with the victim the day before trial. The closer in time to trial you prepare the victim for trial, the greater chance you risk the victim being unable to retell her truth with emotion.

Keep in mind that prepping is NOT coaching. You are allowed to discuss and show any prior statement if the victim forgets something or gets confused. The crimes are likely traumatic events that happened several months, if not years, before the trial. In addition, in interpersonal violence cases, trial requires the victim to remember times, dates, and full details of numerous assaults, sometimes over a period of years. The details of each can confuse the victim, who may be coping with trauma while testifying. You must empower the victim to tell you when the question is confusing or misleading.

The prosecutor should particularly empower the victim to challenge the defense counsel on confusing questions respectfully. A common defense strategy is to ask compound questions that involve different answers and cannot necessarily be answered in a yes or no manner. Give the victim permission to say, "I'm sorry, I don't understand what you are asking," or "I want to answer your questions, but I cannot honestly answer those questions as asked." In preparing the victim for trial, have a colleague step into the role of defense counsel to practice defense objections. This is helpful for the victim and the prosecutor conducting the victim's direct examination. It ensures that not only will the victim be prepared for the many objections that will inevitably occur but the victim will also prepare the prosecutor to consider and talk through their responses in a safe space, not for the first time in the trial. The colleague can also play defense with the victim in prep, giving the victim an idea of what might be asked at trial.

Another best practice is to avoid asking any witness, especially the victim, about time and/or space. There are few times when time or distance matters in intimate violence cases. Time may matter if there is an alibi defense, but this is uncommon in these cases. It is tempting to ask "how long" something lasted to magnify the horrific experience of a victim being assaulted. However, this is a trap that the defense can reverse on the victim.

When you contemplate asking a victim about time and space, ask yourself – does it further your theory or theme or prove an element? If the answer is no, then do not ask. People, in general, are terrible at estimating time. Perception of time is highly relative. Everyone knows that microwave or treadmill minutes are longer than regular minutes! Compare those minutes to snooze button minutes, which are much shorter. A victim's perception of time is naturally unreliable. Compound this with the experience of being in terror and pain. For most victims, the assault lasted an eternity.

If you ask the victim about time, you set her up for impeachment later. For instance, if you ask the victim how long the assault in the bedroom lasted and she says twenty minutes, it becomes very problematic if some texts or calls happened after ten minutes. It is just another area the defense can attack when it is not necessary. The same is true of estimating space. If you need to establish a distance, ask the victim to show you how far away the person is and then actually measure it. If it is a shorter distance, ask different questions rather than "how far away was" the offender. Ask whether the victim would have been able to touch the offender with an arm outstretched. This type of question avoids committing the victim to a specific number but puts the assailant's proximity (if it is a salient fact) into context for the jury.

There may be cases when the victim has specific knowledge of time or distance. If the victim volunteers this in interviews, it could be powerful. For instance, one victim reported that she knew specifically how long it took for her husband to rape her. She watched the clock through the assault, internally praying that the bus would be late, so kids would not come home from school on time. This powerful fact could profoundly impact the jury's ability to understand the victim's experience.

Finally, be cautious during prep about what you discuss while the victim is on the stand. Prosecutors like to familiarize the victim with the courtroom when possible. However, do not joke around or bring up inadmissible information while the victim sits in the witness chair. If you do, you are teaching the victim that she can discuss inappropriate things during testimony. We have seen victims bring up problematic or inadmissible information at trial when the prosecutor has allowed the victim to talk freely on the stand during prep. If you need to explore or discuss things that you will not present at trial, move the witness from the witness chair or even the courtroom before doing so. The witness needs to understand that the witness's job is to answer the questions honestly, and only the questions asked by the attorney.

Soft Cross of the Non-cooperative Victim

Soft cross-examination is a type of cross-examination that can be particularly effective in cases of intimate violence when the victim is no longer cooperating with the prosecution. In a traditional cross-examination, the goal is to impeach the witness's credibility by challenging, disparaging, and impugning the witness' character to create doubt about the testimony. However, in the case where the victim of the crime is not cooperating, recanting, or testifying for the defense, it becomes more complicated. A traditional cross-examination will not work. In many aspects, the prosecutor is still on the victim's side and also needs testimony from the witness. You need the jury to believe that the victim told the truth in the original report. If you go after her using a traditional cross, you signal to the jury that she is a liar. The prosecutor may benefit from the victim's testimony in other ways, like getting out corroborating evidence.

The prosecutor must be aware of the cross's effect on the jury. Again, how the questions are asked has an impact. A jury may develop a dislike for a prosecutor who is seen as attacking someone they are presenting as a victim. The jury may become biased against a victim the prosecutor is trying to protect. A soft cross-examination uses the closed question technique to introduce information or to extract information that reveals to the jury why the victim may not be cooperating, as well as biases, love, fear, or loyalty. In questioning a victim of intimate violence, a soft cross might focus on the control tactics of the defendant, the victim's lack of resources, and the collateral financial and emotional losses that the victim is facing. Soft cross allows you to demonstrate and then educate the panel about the complex issues that arise in intimate violence cases. The prosecutor is not the victim's enemy but an empathic trier of facts and law.

Here is a demonstration of how a soft cross may work. Be mindful of adopting a non-confrontational tone and pace. Assume non-confrontational body language. The prosecutor's approach to the cross communicates to the jury that the victim is sympathetic, and that there are reasons she is not cooperating. She is not an adversary but a victim in an untenable situation.

Start with non-threatening questions.

- What's your relationship?
- Where did you meet?
- What attracted you?
- First date, Proposal, Most romantic gesture
- How quickly did you have kids?
- What is your education level?
- Were you able to work?
- Is he the head of the household in terms of managing the finances, insurance, bank accounts?

Put the victim at ease by allowing her to testify about comfortable topics while you compile testimony that enables you to explain the victim's lack of cooperation in closing. The victim is minimizing or recanting because she has few choices based on the defendant's control of her. She does not want her children's father to go to jail because he is a "great dad." Her lack of cooperation is understandable. It also shows the jury that you are not judging her. Her testimony can be the basis for calling an expert to explain why a victim may minimize or recant.

The next step is to transition to undisputed facts that are non-threatening but reiterates evidence and information from the original police report.

- Did law enforcement come to house/apt?
- Was that at (address)?

- Was that on (date)?
- Was that around (time)?
- How many officers?
- Was suspect home?
- Did LE speak to you/suspect?
- Did they take photographs?
- Collect evidence?
- Call for medical assistance?

Again, show the jury you are not judging the victim's choices. The victim's testimony can corroborate the accuracy of the police report and demonstrates the victim agrees with the report's details.

The next step is if, and then how, you ask the victim questions about the assault. You must consider if you can prove all the elements through other witnesses, such as through hearsay exceptions through first responders or other witnesses. Also, consider what other evidence helps prove any element. Do you have physical evidence, such as a picture of the injuries, to prove the element of bodily harm? Is there a security/Ring camera that can show how the assault occurred? Are there texts of social media posts that contain admissions by the defendant? The less you must question the victim about the actual assault, the less likely she will feel the need to recant or minimize.

If you must ask about the assault, tread lightly. It may just be getting her to confirm that she did indeed tell the police what is contained in the report. If necessary, you may put on an expert to "educate" the jury about the victim's counter-intuitive behaviors, such as why victims stay and recant. Using the "power and control" wheel is helpful as a demonstrative. The expert can also speak to the complexities of emotions, from love and fear to one of the most powerful, hope. The prosecutor can utilize this testimony in closing and rebuttal to argue that the victim told the truth night she reported. Still, because of the defendant's influence or her inability to provide for the children, she is now recanting or minimizing.

There are two approaches to the soft cross of a victim who is not cooperating with the prosecution. The prosecutor can call her in the case in chief and just ask fundamental or background questions. Although this is not really a cross, the prosecutor may have to have the victim declared a hostile witness. This gives you the latitude to ask more leading questions. Calling the victim a witness, even simply to corroborate basic facts, may allow the prosecutor to put on other witnesses because the Confrontation Clause will have been satisfied. Now, the prosecutor can put on a first responder to testify to an excited utterance made by the victim. You can also do an actual soft cross if the victim is testifying for the defense.

Cross-examination of the Intimate Violence Defendant

The point of traditional cross-examination is to impeach the credibility of the witness. A few basic approaches can lead to a successful cross, starting with questions that are single-fact and leading. Begin your interaction with the offender showing the jury (and defendant) you are in control. Sometimes, with a defendant that is used to being in control or talking his way out of trouble, this experience will be disconcerting and anxiety-provoking. The prosecutor must be well prepared to impeach.

This could be challenging when planning and executing the cross of a defendant if they invoked or requested a lawyer. How can you possibly prepare a cross of a defendant if there are no written or recorded statements to law enforcement? You can, but you need to plan and know where to look. For instance, you must not only acquire every police report but also interview the police officers that took those statements. Maybe the defendant said something on the scene that investigators did not record in the report. You must also interview co-workers, neighbors, friends, and family to capture ANY statement the defendant made, whether inculpatory or exculpatory. Other possible sources of statements are text messages, social media, and jailhouse phone calls.

The cross of the defendant must be organized and contain relevant information to be effective. Just like every other part of the trial, primacy and recency are key in the presentation of information. The prosecutor should be in charge and not afraid to address difficult issues. This is the reason for short, one-fact questions. It is difficult for the offender to go on a diatribe from the stand if he can answer the question yes or no. Limiting the offender's ability to deny, explain, or change the evidence is critical.

Another approach that may be successful is not to do a chronological cross. The defendant will be well prepared to answer questions chronologically. However, if you can conduct a cross that is not necessarily chronological, you may gain the upper hand. The defendant loses control of the script; his testimony may not come off as smoothly as he rehearsed. If you are going to jump around chronologically, you must ensure that it is clear to the jury.

The best way to stay focused is through chapters. Some common chapters in intimate violence cases include:

- Size difference

  - You're 6'4"
  - She's 5'2"
  - You're infantry
  - She's a stay-at-home mom
  - You work out every day
  - You max the fitness test every year
  - She doesn't work out
  - You lift 250 lbs.
  - She weighs 100 lbs.

- Physical evidence

  - Her left eye was black
  - You're right-handed
  - Your right hand was bleeding
  - Your right hand was swollen
  - She was crying
  - She was breathing heavy
  - She called the police.

- Prior statements

  - In your direct examination you said that the victim attacked you first and you were acting in self-defense
  - You gave a statement to the police
  - You knew it was important to tell them everything that occurred that night?
  - You wrote a three-page statement

- They allowed you to review and add or cross out anything that wasn't the truth?
- In fact, this is your signature?
- And these are your initials on the end of every page
- And you acknowledged that this statement was under the penalty of perjury
- But you told the police on the night you were arrested that you never struck your wife
- In fact, you told them you had no idea how she got the black eye

- Choices

  - Could have walked away
  - Gone to another room
  - Locked the door
  - Left house
  - Called 911
  - Contrast violence
  - She slapped you?
  - You punched her?
  - She kicked you?
  - You threw her to the ground?
  - Then you strangled her?
  - She punched you?
  - You stabbed her?

- Confront with evidence

  - 911 call
  - Photos
  - Other witness testimony
  - Medical evidence
  - Text messages
  - SM posts
  - Apology cards/presents

The other aspect of a powerful cross is being prepared to AND know how to properly execute impeachment. This should guide the questions you ask. Do not ask a question the defendant can deny without the evidence to impeach him. For instance, do not ask a question about whether the defendant threatened the victim (which he can easily deny) UNLESS you have evidence that refutes his denial. It may come in the form of a text message which contains the threat, a law enforcement interview where the defendant admitted the threat, or a witness who actually heard the threat.

Intimate violence offenders are particularly confident, ego-centric, and do not like being controlled. They will try to deflect, explain, and pontificate while answering a yes or no question. Do not let that happen. There are a few methods that you can employ to take control back from an offender who attempts to dominate the testimony. First, if the defendant does try to elaborate, do not seek help from the judge; take control back yourself. You can stop him once he says more than yes or no by interrupting him and asking if he understood the question. Then ask the question again. If he persists, another method is to put your hand up in a stop motion (think talk to the hand) and look away, signaling to the jury to stop paying attention to him.

Cross-examination is not long, hard-fought battle; it is a raid. You must get in and get out by using focused single-fact questions which prove your theory and shows the defendant is being, at best, disingenuous or, at worst, a liar. Remember that a well-done cross will lose effectiveness if you do not remind the jury in closing and/or rebuttal about what the defendant did, said, or did not say.

Expert Testimony

F.R.E 702 defines an expert witness as someone with specialized knowledge, skill, experience, or education. Intimate violence cases can always benefit from at least an expert consultant. Analyze your case carefully and identify the need for expertise early. A prosecutor first formulates theme/theory and then works with an expert to refine it. You must think critically when determining the appropriate expert and their usefulness. Do not overlook the impact of an expert in educating a jury and advising their decision-making, especially in the cases of intimate violence where biases and myths abound. Additionally, do not assume the judge's or jury's "common sense" includes knowledge about intimate violence.

Once you determine that you need an expert, you need to determine who is best for the facts of your case. It must be the best person possible who is suited for the subject and does not have any investment in the case. The entire point of experts is that they are unbiased and form opinions based on science and facts. An expert should have the appropriate education and experience but also be articulate, personable, and able to communicate concepts effectively. Once you decide to get an expert, do not assume the judge understands the law or the science involved. Be prepared to educate the judge regarding your need for an expert through the use of pre-trial motions. Also, be prepared to understand when you need to argue against the defense's use of experts.

Although there is a relatively low standard for qualifying an expert, you need to understand the law that sets those standards. The law differs depending on what type of expert you are qualifying for. For "hard science" experts (e.g., DNA, medical), you must apply the standards for the expert testimony as defined in *Daubert v. Merrell Dow Pharmaceuticals, Inc.*, 509 U.S. 579 (1993). The standard for expert testimony asks:

- Whether the theory/technique can be and has been tested
- Whether theory/technique has been subjected to peer review and/or publication
- If there is a known and acceptable potential error rate
- Whether the theory/technique has general acceptance within the scientific community

The range of potential "hard science" experts in intimate violence cases include toxicology, DNA, Sexual Assault Forensic Examiner/Medical Forensic Examiner, Doctors, Digital Forensic Examiner, Ballistics Experts, or others. The most common expert in intimate violence is a medical expert. Medical experts can testify about physical abuse and whether the injuries are consistent or inconsistent with the history provided. They can testify about how injuries are caused or the degree of force, or refute claims of easy bruising or alternative causes of injuries. A medical expert can negate the belief that bruises can be dated.

In sexual assault cases, the medical provider, including a SANE nurse of Sexual Assault Medical Forensic Examiner, can testify to the anatomy, so the jury understands the names and locations of the genitalia. They can testify to what the physical findings or lack thereof mean. For strangulation cases, the medical provider can explain the affected anatomy and organs. They can describe the physiological effects of strangulation and injury/lack of injury. The medical expert can testify to whether the strangulation caused grievous bodily harm (GBH) or means likely to cause GBH or death, should your statute necessitate either. Medical experts should never testify without a review of the case file and evidence. They should always be assisting the prosecutor in understanding the medical records and helping prepare the cross of the defense expert.

For "soft science" experts, like a forensic psychologist or victim advocate, the prosecutor must apply the test set forth by the court in *Kumho Tire v. Patrick Carmichael*, 526 U.S. 137 (1999). It applies *the Daubert* standard to non-scientific evidence and "reliability" is the key to determination. If you are practicing in military courts, you should apply the test in *U.S. v. Houser, 36 M.J. 392 (C.M.A. 1993)* for soft science experts. The Houser test has six prongs:

- Qualifications of the expert;
- Proper Subject Matter for expert testimony;
- Proper basis for expert opinion & testimony;
- Relevance (MRE 401);
- Reliability (MRE 702);
- Probative value of the opinion (MRE 403).

Soft science experts' testimony is generally psychological or sociological in nature. They traditionally testify to typical reactions to domestic violence/sexual assault by victims before, during, and after incidents, educating juries on victim response and demystifying misinformation about victims of domestic or sexual violence. If qualified, the expert might testify on memory and recall, especially as impacted by trauma. They can explain why victims stay or recant. Some experts could be used in sentencing to discuss an offender's rehabilitation potential for sentencing.

There are some limitations to expert testimony involving victim behavior. An expert can never testify about victim credibility or comment on "signs" of truthfulness or deception. The expert's testimony is NOT BOLSTERING. The expert is not telling the factfinder to believe the victim. The expert is providing education so that the factfinder does not DISBELIEVE the victim because of myths. The expert can dispel "DV and rape myths" often held by many in the community and lead the jury/judge to doubt the victim's credibility inaccurately. One way around the "human lie detector objection having a blind expert so that the expert cannot be accused of bias because the expert has no specific knowledge about the case. You may want to use a blind expert if you are trying to explain the effects of trauma on the brain to the jury. But you may not want to keep your expert blind if you want them involved in victim/witness preparation and helping with other aspects of the case. In that case, if the expert does testify, ensure the expert understands the need to provide general education, not tailored to meet the facts of the case.

Cross of the soft science expert is usually focused on the fact that no "diagnostic tool" exists to determine the validity of accusation, that victims lie, and that the research and information they base their opinions on are self-reported. Your expert must be ready to concede these points. The prosecutor must be prepared to re-direct the expert about other sciences that are based on self-report, such as diagnosing most psychological disorders like posttraumatic stress disorder.

Once you have decided that you need an expert and have found the right expert, your work has just begun. Before meeting with the expert, you must prepare. If your expert is not blind, you must review all the material and ensure that your expert has the same information and materials. Additionally, you must ensure that your expert has everything the prosecutor provides to the defense and vice versa. You will be unable to prepare a proper direct from the expert unless you understand the facts as they relate to the science. The prosecutor must be aware of the distinctions in the information and how it is used. The prosecutor must know all the information to ask the right questions and understand evidence. The prosecutor shares less information with the jury. Finally, the prosecutor must know additional information, often provided by the expert, to prevent unfair or misleading cross-examination.

When preparing your expert for trial, you must take steps to ensure that you are maximizing their time while educating yourself. Go to where they are if possible. Prepare them in person. Ask about their methodology and background. Get them to help you anticipate the issues associated with your theory or how the science does not necessarily support the theory. Google your own expert to see what information they are giving the public and what others are saying about them. Cover any possible "landmines," either personal or professional, that might be raised in cross-examination, like ethics violations or findings of professional misconduct. Encourage the expert's willingness to communicate with the defense attorney to prepare. In general, avoid "joint" meetings with defense to prepare the expert, even if the expert prefers it.

Before you put an expert on the stand, you must decide the purpose of the expert testimony and how you will use this evidence in closing. You may make a last-minute decision to have your expert not testify at all. If your expert is necessary to explain facts or science or prove an element, then, clearly, they must testify in your case in chief. If your expert only needs to testify about a defense expert's testimony, then they will testify in rebuttal. The last-minute decision as to whether the expert testifies often depends on whether the defense expert testifies or whether you were able to neutralize or co-opt their opinion sufficiently in cross-examination. Having an expert present can manage a defense expert willing to go outside the lines or beyond the science.

As a former state prosecutor, I am painfully aware that there is rarely money in the budget to acquire a paid expert. However, you can mine your experts for low or no cost. Often a local woman's shelter will have an advocate that will testify about domestic violence dynamics. Local emergency room doctors may be able to testify about injury. Clinic doctors can testify about anatomy. Universities may have experts they will allow to testify at low or no cost. State police or FBI may have professional resources for toxicology or other physical evidence. Your state's domestic violence or sexual assault agency may have resources to recommend.

Closing Argument

A closing argument must consist of at least four components. These include the attention step; the elements of the crime and the facts that prove them beyond a reasonable doubt; jury instructions; and finally, the exit line. As in the opening statement, the attention step needs to hook the jury and leave them wanting to hear more. Most commonly, a powerful direct quote from the defendant, victim, or witness or a compelling theme can be an effective attention-getter. You may also consider using evidence such as a picture of injuries, autopsy photos, or crime scene photos. Displaying the weapon used can grab the jury's attention. Contrasting two photos of the victim, how she appeared before the destruction the defendant unleashed, then after.

A powerful theme in an intimate violence case may be "His Weapon of Choice: Her Trust." The following is an example of incorporating the theme into the closing.

The weapon used against Ms. Smith wasn't a gun or a knife. Those you can see. The defendant, her superior, used a more dangerous weapon against her. It is a weapon that you cannot see coming and by the time you realize it is being used against you – it is too late. That weapon was her trust. You see, he used her own trust to isolate her, get her alone, and then even question herself about what he had done. He counted on the fact that she trusted him when he told her she was like a daughter to him. He counted on the fact that she trusted him when he kept telling her he would get her home safely. But most importantly he used her trust in the most manipulative way possible when he completely betrayed her trust by pretending the next day that he was so sorry that she was upset, because she had definitely hit on him and actually was the aggressor.

The body of the closing argument contains two essential components. First, you need to convince the jury that the victim and prosecution witnesses are credible and the defendant and defense witnesses were not credible (or their evidence was meaningless). You need to explain each offense's elements and demonstrate how the evidence proves each of them by weaving the law (elements and jury instructions) into the facts. Common jury instructions in intimate violence cases include instructions regarding the credibility of witnesses, consent or mistake of fact as to consent, self-defense, and reasonable doubt. The prosecution must embrace the elements and the issue of consent (that there was none or he could not have been mistaken) instructions in the opening close. A best practice is to leave credibility and reasonable doubt for rebuttal. Those are topics when you want the last word. Just like in the opening, do not address or "chase" the defense during your opening close. This is your chance to frame your case the way you want the jury to understand it in the deliberation room. If you try to "prebutt" the defense's theory in your opening close, you simply give them the chance to answer in their own close. If you put forth your theme, the facts that support your theory, and how the law supports both into your opening close, the defense will have to argue their theory and argue against yours. That allows you to have the last word in rebuttal when you tell the jury why the defense's theory is either not reasonable or devoid of facts to support their theory or they are improperly applying the law.

In keeping with the concept of primacy and recency, the exit line is just as important as the attention-getter. Prosecutors love to end their closing with their prayer for relief. You cannot spend time and effort writing a compelling and powerful closing argument only to end on a sentence that is neither powerful nor compelling. The prayer for relief usually sounds something like this: "Now that you have heard all the evidence presented, the Government is confident that we have proved every charge beyond a reasonable doubt and that you will come back with the only verdict supported by the evidence. That verdict is that the defendant is guilty of all charges. Thank you." You certainly want to ask the jury for what you want but ask for the finding of guilt BEFORE you end your argument. After you explain how your evidence supports the charges, then ask for your prayer for relief. Your exit line should be your theme. For example:

The government asks that you find the only verdict that is warranted and that is a verdict of guilty. Because Ms. Jones is going back the house tonight. A house where she was abused, terrorized, disparaged, and had her trust destroyed. But worst of all, it became the house of secrets because she was told 'if you tell anyone no one will believe you' and 'I will make sure you never see the kids.' And that threat kept her quiet for years. Until she couldn't live in the house of secrets anymore. Your verdict will show her she doesn't have to keep secrets anymore and that she can sleep tonight knowing she and her children can make that house a home.

The way you present your closing is as important as the substance of your closing. Be a storyteller preaching to the infidels as well as the choir, but give the choir some lyrics. Use your voice, eye contact, and mannerisms to highlight your strengths. This can include pausing when you want the jury to ruminate on a point or modulating your voice to emphasize a certain point. Attend to how you move around the courtroom. Many prosecutors simply pace, which can be unintentional but also distracting. Move about the courtroom with a purpose. For instance, you may want to move over to the defense table when you are describing in detail how the defendant abused the victim or move to the witness stand when you are recounting the detailed and emotional testimony of the victim.

The use of technology in closing is not necessary but can be compelling. It does not need to dominate your actual argument, nor should it. Slides or visuals should be used to summarize complicated elements and instructions or heighten evidence (photos, quotes, timelines) that you want the jury to remember and review in deliberations. Some examples of the use of technology are available in Appendix D.

Rebuttal

Rebuttal argument is your last chance to persuade the jury. The government is entitled to rebuttal because it bears the burden of proof. Keep the rebuttal short and sweet. Do not attempt to rebut every point the defense made, as tempting as it may be. The attention span of most people is not long. If you take them through your closing again or try and answer all the defense's points, the most powerful points will be lost. And by rebutting each point, you are giving the defense argument more weight than it deserves.

You must prepare a rebuttal in advance. You may use some or none of it, but you must be thinking ahead of time about how you will counter the defense argument. First, you should have an idea of what the defense is before trial even starts. Even if you are not certain you can prepare for the two or three arguments you think it might be. You will certainly know their defense after their opening statement. Therefore, you can concentrate on that rebuttal as the trial unfolds.

Depending on the complexity of the case you should keep your rebuttal points to a minimum. For a straightforward case, you should pick your top three points. If the case has many charges, maybe that number goes up. Even though you have already "prepared" a rebuttal, make a list of points you think the defense made during their closing, then pick the top three or four points that need to be rebutted. Some points may be on your prepared rebuttal, but do not be afraid to use all new points if you feel they had the biggest impact on the jury and need to be negated.

Sentencing

Sentencing should not be an afterthought. You should think about sentencing from the time you get the case file. What is the case worth? Honestly and realistically assess it. Talk to witnesses – especially the victim – about the impact of the crimes during your initial interviews with them. This will help you honestly assess the worth of the case.

Wargame out the possibilities ahead of time. If the accused is found guilty of a lesser offense and not the gravamen, what will you argue? If the accused is convicted of everything except something like obstruction of justice, what are you going to argue? Think about your theme and the evidence you will admit in sentencing BEFORE TRIAL. Consider the defense's approach and how you will attack it. Is the defendant famous, powerful, wealthy, or part of the system? What doors will they open?

Because sentencing rules vary greatly from state to state, federal, and military, I will discuss the goals of sentencing in broad terms. Your sentencing theme needs to highlight important aspects of your case for the sentencing authority. Consider highlighting the purposefulness of the accused's actions, vulnerability of the victims, matters in aggravation, minimize extenuation and mitigation, rehabilitative potential, general and specific deterrence and, for the military, good order and discipline. Consider how you want to present your sentencing case regarding victim

impact. Does your victim want to give sworn testimony or express her feelings in a victim impact statement? Either way, it occurs, you want to prepare your victim so that the entire impact
of the crime is felt. Appendix E provides recommendations on how to interview the victim for
sentencing.

Summary

Trial is arduous and complex. This chapter's goal was to provide some practical strategies for dealing with cases of intimate violence. From opening to rebuttal, an offender-focused theme helps
the prosecutor navigate the complicated terrain of these cases. Throughout the case, the prosecutor must be flexible, responding proactively to the witness testimony and evolving evidence. In
conclusion,

- Preparation is critical, as is adaptability.
- There is the need to modify more traditional approaches to direct and cross-examination to
  capture the complexity and subtlety of intimate violence cases.
- The prosecutor must remain aware of what the prosecutor projects regarding the victim. The
  wrong tone, questions, or body language can transmit doubt and judgment of the victim to
  the jury.
- Experts may play a more significant role in cases of intimate violence than in other cases.
- An offender focus must permeate all stages of the trial to keep the factfinders' attention on the
  appropriate party – the defendant.

References

Bugliosi, V. (1996). *Outrage: The five reasons why O. J. Simpson got away with murder.* W. W. Norton &
  Company.
Daubert v. Merrel Dow Pharmaceuticals, Inc., 509 U.S. 579 (1993). https://supreme.justia.com/cases/
  federal/us/509/579/
Kumho Tire v. Patrick Carmichael, 526 U.S. 137 (1999). https://supreme.justia.com/cases/federal/
  us/526/137/
United States v. Houser, 36 M.J. 392 (1993). https://cite.case.law/mj/36/392/

Chapter 11

Evidence-Based Prosecution

There are countless reasons why a victim may choose not to participate in the prosecution of the accused. Many people ask, "Why should you try a case without the victim? If she doesn't care, why should we?" These are questions law enforcement, prosecutors, jurors, and even judges constantly ask in intimate violence cases. In reality, prosecutors try cases every day in the criminal justice system without a victim – it's called murder. But there are many other instances of cases being brought when the victim cannot testify, like cases of abuse of very young children, elder abuse, and abuse of people with disabilities that make them unable to communicate. How? We gather evidence. In murder cases, where there is no victim to talk to, we find evidence to prove what happened to that person.

The difference between cases where a victim cannot tell law enforcement what happened and a person that can testify but chooses not to is nuanced. Throughout this book, we have outlined reasons a victim may not cooperate and recommendations for increasing the odds that the victim will participate and cooperate. However, the recantation by and dropout rate of victims of intimate violence remains high, especially in cases when the victim has a relationship with the perpetrator. Therefore, every investigation and potential prosecution of intimate crimes should be conducted as if the victim will recant or even testify for the defense. This type of prosecution has very accurately been called evidence-based prosecution for decades.

What Is Evidence-Based Prosecution?

Evidence-based prosecution is an approach whereby prosecutors build a case based on available evidence, irrespective of the victim's willingness to participate in the case or testify against their abuser. This approach began around the mid-1980s and early 1990s in communities such as Duluth, Minnesota, San Diego and Los Angeles, California, and Nashville, Tennessee. The fundamental principle of evidence-based prosecution is that provable domestic violence cases should be prosecuted irrespective of whether the victim is cooperative or willing to participate in the case (Gwinn & O'Dell, 1992). While there are many caveats to going forward with an evidence-based prosecution with an unwilling victim, a prosecutor must be willing to approach cases of intimate violence as if they will go forward and be prepared for the case.

Throughout this chapter, we will primarily focus on using evidence-based prosecution in prosecuting intimate partner or domestic violence cases. However, prosecutors can use this type of prosecution in other cases of intimate violence. Intellectually disabled individuals, especially non-verbal, have a very difficult time providing testimony, but are at significantly greater risk of sexual and physical abuse (National Coalition Against Domestic Violence [NCADV], n.d.). The same is true for the elderly, young children, the mentally ill, and other populations

DOI: 10.4324/9781003121855-14

that would have difficulty providing testimony in court. Evidence-based prosecution should be considered in all cases when a victim may not be available or be able to give testimony for various reasons.

Why We Should Care

Intimate partner violence has devastating effects on the victim, children, families, and society. The offenders are lethal and have far-reaching impacts. Statistics provided by the NCADV (n.d.) show:

- Offenders of intimate partner violence are the single largest cause of injury to women between 15 and 44.
- One out of four women is severely abused by an intimate partner.
- One in two female homicide victims is killed by an intimate partner. Intimate partner offenders commit over 70% of murder-suicides. Twenty percent of the homicide victims of these offenders are family, friends, law enforcement, or bystanders.
- Intimate partner violence accounts for 15% of all crime.
- Pregnant women are more likely to die of homicide by an intimate partner than any other cause.
- Half of domestic violence offenders also assault their children.
- Victims of intimate violence experience serious injury, significant detrimental psychological effects, and damaging economic consequences, including loss of work days and employment.

Domestic violence victimizes everyone in the household, not just the battered spouse. As many as ten million children and teens witness violence between their caretakers annually (American Academy of Child and Adolescent Psychiatry, 2019). They experience child abuse at a rate 15 times higher than average and witness a vast majority of the violent events (NCADV, n.d.). Children exposed to domestic violence have an increased risk of developing significant emotional and behavioral issues, as well as serious health problems as an adult (NCADV, n.d.). The battering parent typically demonstrates a dysfunctional parenting style that provides distorted role modeling and disrupts and undermines the children's relationship with the battered parent (Bancroft et al., 2012). Children exposed to domestic violence are at significant risk of generationally transmitting the trauma, either by becoming abusers or victims (Lunnemann et al., 2019).

Domestic violence perpetrators are not only destructive to the victim and their children but they also affect neighbors, bystanders, animals, law enforcement, and anyone in the wrong place at the wrong time. There is a significant link between interpersonal violence and animal abuse (Robinson & Clausen, 2021). Domestic violence offenders pose a dire risk to our community, as well as to their families.

The wish to murder his wife was the impetus for the D. C. Sniper (Dvorak, 2022). John Allen Muhammad (a/k/a the D. C. Sniper) caused panic and terror throughout Maryland, Virginia, and the District of Columbia by randomly shooting 13 people, killing ten. Most do not know the motive behind these murders. Before the killing spree, Muhammad's wife had escaped him after years of horrible abuse; she was afraid he would kill her. He had threatened to kill her; she "knew he was going to shoot [her] in the head." She obtained a protective order in the state of Washington, then moved across the country to Maryland. After learning his wife left him when he was served with the protective order, he decided to kill her. However, Muhammad was smart enough to know he would be the primary suspect in her murder, especially after she obtained a protective order. Muhammad enacted a plan to ensure the police would never suspect him. He would randomly shoot strangers, then eventually kill his ex-wife. Luckily for her, he was caught before he had the chance to kill her.

The majority of mass shooters have a history of domestic violence. These shootings include the Las Vegas Massacre, the Pulse Nightclub shooting, the Virginia Tech Massacre, the shooting at Sandy Hook, and more. A recent analysis of mass shootings revealed that nearly 70% of mass shooters have a history of domestic violence (Geller et al., 2021). Not only do most mass shooters have a history of domestic violence perpetration but those that do are also more lethal, attaining higher fatality rates in their mass shootings than those without a history of domestic violence. Domestic violence offenders pose a serious risk to police officers. According to the FBI's Law Enforcement Killed and Assaulted (LEOKA) database, 503 officers nationwide were killed between 2011 and 2020. During that period, 43 officers (8.5%) were killed by responding to domestic violence calls (Tucker, 2022).

When We Should Go Forward with Evidence-Based Prosecution

To decide whether to proceed with an evidence-based prosecution, the prosecutor must first determine whether the case has the evidentiary capacity to go forward. We will discuss this further in this chapter. What the prosecutor must also consider are the victim's circumstances and fears. Consider whether the victim will be worse off than the day before she met you. Is the victim equipped to deal with the consequence of prosecution? You must analyze what effects a conviction may have on the victim. Will the offender, the sole source of income, be facing jail time and be unable to work? Will he lose his job and, therefore, the source of the family's health insurance? The prosecutor must balance these questions with the abuse's severity and the offender's potential lethality. The victim's fear of future bodily harm or death may outweigh the victim's fear of the losses she will face. Sometimes, notwithstanding the victim's wishes, the prosecutor has the responsibility to intervene to hold the offender accountable, protect the victim and society, and potentially deter future acts of violence. The prosecutor has many responsibilities but ultimately, according to Standard 1.1 of the National District Attorneys Association (NDAA, 2009),

> *The prosecutor is an independent administrator of justice. The primary responsibility of a prosecutor is to seek justice, which can only be achieved by the representation and presentation of the truth. This responsibility includes, but is not limited to, ensuring that the guilty are held accountable, that the innocent are protected from unwarranted harm, and that the rights of all participants, particularly victims of crime, are respected.*

(p. 2)

How Far to Go to Produce the Victim

Regarding the victim who will not cooperate, the prosecutor must consider the length you or your boss is willing to go to get a victim into court. Her presence may be necessary for a multitude of reasons. Are you willing to subpoena the victim? How far are you ready to go to ensure the subpoena is honored? Generally, the only way to enforce a subpoena is to have the Judge sign a writ of attachment, allowing law enforcement to take a witness into custody until it is time for testimony. There is significant negative fallout to this approach, for instance, how it looks for the prosecutor's office, how it impacts any future relationship with the victim, and the collateral consequences to the victim for being in custody. If the victim is the children's sole caretaker, the children may end up in the system. If the victim is in custody while the perpetrator is free, this is a contradictory message to all parties.

A more reasonable alternative may be that the prosecutor sends an investigator from the office to explain to the victim what could happen with a writ of attachment. Then, the prosecutor could offer the victim a chance to come to speak with you. The prosecutor can explain the simple and non-incriminating questions the victim needs to answer, like simply identifying the defendant. The prosecutor can assure the victim she will get a chance to talk about the good times in the relationship, allowing her to show the defendant publicly that she is on his side. The prosecutor can then use the information about the relationship to bolster the argument in closing that love keeps her from testifying while pointing out all the things the offender did to manipulate the victim.

The Basis for Charging Decisions

Prosecutors struggle with charging decisions. Many prosecutors falsely believe that they cannot charge a case unless they believe there is a good chance of a conviction. This is a poor basis for charging decisions. In 28 years of prosecuting crimes of intimate violence, this author has rarely based decisions on the probability of conviction. These cases are difficult; acquittals are expected. The case becomes an especially complicated issue when the victim declines to prosecute. The NDAA (2009) also gives guidance on this in Standard 4-2.2,

> *While commencing a prosecution is permitted by most ethical standards upon a determination that probable cause exists to believe that a crime has been committed and that the defendant has committed it, the standard prescribes a higher standard for filing a criminal charge. To suggest that the charging standard should be the prosecutor's reasonable belief that the charges can be substantiated by admissible evidence at trial is recognition of the powerful effects of the initiation of criminal charges.*

(p. 52)

Many prosecutors interpret this as a mandate to believe they can secure a conviction before charging. What this standard does say is that it is ethical to charge a case based on probable cause. The higher standard is that the prosecutor must simply have a *reasonable belief* that a charge could stand with admissible evidence. If the prosecutor believes the victim and can get evidence introduced, whether, through the victim or other means, the prosecutor can charge and prosecute. It should not matter if the victim decides not to testify if the prosecutor has a reasonable belief; the prosecutor can present the evidence in alternative ways.

Who Should Be Prosecuted in Evidence-Based Prosecution

There are many cases that can be prosecuted evidence-based, but not all of them should be. Especially in offender-focused prosecution, the prosecutor should analyze who the offender is and what ultimate danger he may pose to the victim and the public. Does the threat he poses outweigh the wishes and needs of the victim?

This author was once prepared to go to trial on a domestic violence case in Chicago. The defendant was a fire captain; the evidence was solid. The victim came to me and begged me not to prosecute. She was leaving him and was set to get half his pension when he retired later that year. She planned to live off the divorce settlement. Because he was an officer in the fire department, a conviction would mean he would be fired and lose his retirement. I could prosecute him without the victim's participation, but I had to ask myself if he posed a future danger. After a full review of his non-existent criminal history and interviews with the victim, neighbors, and family members, I had my answer. The defendant had been verbally abusive for several years. He had been abusive, pushing and grabbing her by the arm, but not severely violent. There were no other risk factors or indices of lethality. She did not fear he would kill her if she left. The best thing for this victim was to leave him; a conviction would take away the only avenue she had to achieve this. I made the decision to drop the charges, with the possibility of re-filing until the divorce and settlement were final. She sent me Christmas cards for a few years after, updating me on her new life and describing how happy she was to have been able to leave and be free of the abuse.

Another case took a different turn. The defendant was Chicago Housing Authority police officer. He had beaten the victim for an hour wherein she sustained multiple injuries. He then would not allow her to make a phone call or leave the house. She waited until he fell asleep and fled the house, half-clothed in winter. She was able to get to a neighbor's house, who called 911. The police and EMT's responded. She was eventually treated at the ER. The victim was at the bail hearing the next day, begging the judge to drop the charges, saying she had lied about the whole thing. I met with her, explained that I was very worried about her, and did a lethality assessment. I identified how he was abusing in various ways, using the Power and Control wheel. I told her while I respected her decision not to participate, I was not dropping the charges. I determined quickly I could use evidence-based prosecution against the defendant. As time passed, she constantly reached out with her plea to drop the charges. I was in a moral conundrum. He was high risk for lethality. He had other domestic violence arrests and violations of protective orders. I was convinced that if I dropped the charges, he would eventually kill her, but if I did prosecute him, he might kill her. The offender helped me decide. He appeared at my office demanding to speak to me. The offender had escalated, trying to manipulate and intimidate me, revealing another level of entitlement and aggression. I eventually did prosecute and convicted him, using evidence-based prosecution. The victim stayed with him for another year, then left. She called me to say how grateful she was that I went forward. She wanted him to be held accountable, but she did not want to be the one responsible for it.

Besides the severity of the abuse and the offender's risk level, the prosecutor has to consider who the offender is and how much power he wields. Victims experience more helplessness, confusion, and fear when in a relationship with a wealthy or powerful offender. Offenders with money, power, or status know how to leverage these things to avoid accountability and get out of trouble. They have proven this to the victim as well. In addition, these offenders have allies that support and validate the offender, proving to the victim his influence. These allies may also blame the victim for the offender's actions.

Jennie Willoughby (2017), in her blog post "Why I Stayed," articulates the dilemma of being abused by a powerful man artfully. Jennie Willoughby is the ex-wife of Rob Porter, one of the top advisers to then-President Trump. He had abused his ex-wife for years. She never told anyone because she feared what he might do to her. Once she divorced him and was able to get some distance, she wrote a blog about her situation. Part of her blog explains,

> When I tried to get help, I was counseled to consider carefully how what I said might affect his career. And so, I kept my mouth shut and stayed. I was told, yes, he was deeply flawed, but then again so was I. And so, I worked on myself and stayed. If he was a monster all the time, perhaps it would have been easier to leave. But he could be kind and sensitive. And so, I stayed. He belittled my intelligence and destroyed my confidence. And so, I stayed. I felt ashamed and trapped. And so, I stayed. Friends and clergy didn't believe me. And so, I stayed. I was pregnant. And so, I stayed. I lost the pregnancy and became depressed. And so, I stayed.

There are many things to consider when deciding whether to do an evidence-based prosecution. There is a fine line between balancing the victim's wishes and truly analyzing the dangerousness and power that an offender possesses. Remember that it is always possible that the victim wants the system to step and take over. The key is ensuring you are listening and verifying the victim's concerns to make the right decision.

How to Do Evidence-Based Prosecution

How do you assemble an evidence-based prosecution? In a nutshell, these are the basic steps you need to take to construct a solid case. This section will discuss each step in depth to provide the tips you need to prosecute a case evidence-based successfully.

Work with Law Enforcement to Gather the Evidence You Need

While we have discussed the importance of working with law enforcement in a previous chapter, it bears repeating. The prosecutor can form a strong alliance and reliance on their law enforcement team. Teach law enforcement about what an evidence-based prosecution is. Our experience is that prosecutors and law officers become frustrated and hopeless about working with victims of domestic violence. They become apathetic about cases that they are invested in but come to no fruition. Working together to gather evidence to decrease the case's reliance on the victim's cooperation can invigorate and motivate the investigating officers. The prosecutor must educate law enforcement about what evidence is needed, why it is needed, how to get it quickly, and where to look. For both first responders and investigators, some prosecutors have developed a general checklist to guide what to ask and what to look for during investigations.

Analyze the Admissibility of the Victim's Statements

The prosecutor must understand, then master the rules of evidence, especially hearsay, to determine whether you can litigate an evidence-based prosecution. First, it is important to understand what is NOT hearsay. The Federal Rules of Evidence (2020) describe hearsay in rule 801. FRE 801 states:

(1)(A) Prior inconsistent statement made under oath and subject to cross;
(1)(B) Prior consistent statements when

    (i)   motive to fabricate postdates statement OR
    (ii) anytime a declarant's credibility is attacked to rebut that inference;

(2) Statements of a party opponent.

It is essential to understand this rule for a few reasons. First, you may be able to use statements made by the victim in earlier hearings, like when the victim is on the stand and fully cross-examined in preliminary hearings. If the victim refuses to testify or recants on the stand, you can use that testimony as a prior consistent statement. Second, you must understand 801(1)(B). This rule becomes relevant if the victim testifies partially truthfully or decides last minute that she wants to participate in the trial. Victims do decide to participate late in trial, especially when they tire of harassment and lies or experience more abuse. If the prosecutor has kept the lines of communication open with the victim, she is more likely to reach out or agree to participate late in the process.

The rule regarding hearsay has several exceptions that become highly relevant in evidence-based prosecution. You must determine whether any hearsay exceptions apply and how you can present them in court. FRE 803 describes hearsay exceptions, which include:

- Present Sense Impression
- Excited Utterance
- Then Existing Mental, Emotional, or Physical Condition
- Statements for Medical Diagnosis or Treatment
- Records of Regularly Conducted Activity

Effect on the listener is not a hearsay exception but is an argument prosecutors often rely upon to admit witness statements. We will discuss this argument below.

Present Sense Impression

A present sense impression is a spontaneous statement made by someone that describes or explains an event or condition, made during an event or immediately after the declarant perceived it. This exception differs from excited utterance because the declarant is not required to be excited. Timing of the statement is the key to whether a statement fits under the present sense impression. The statement must come during or immediately after the event. 911 calls are good sources of present sense impressions as the caller is describing events as they are unfolding. This exception comes under the most significant judicial scrutiny as some argue that it does not possess the guarantee of trustworthiness of other exceptions. A best practice is to rely on this exception last.

Excited Utterance

An excited utterance is a statement relating to a startling event or condition, made while the declarant was under the stress of excitement that it caused. State case law varies, but depending on the circumstances, the outer limit of elapsed time is thirty to forty-five minutes from the event. In many states, there is a longer time period for children. Be sure to check the case law in your state to determine what time limits dictate the definition of excited utterance for adults and children.

One of the challenges of evidence-based prosecution is laying the foundation for this exception without the victim. One option is to use the first responders or a witness who heard the victim's statement. Remember, you can elicit hearsay to establish a foundation. Perhaps the victim told the witness, "I called you right after he hit me and left." This statement can be used to establish the time elapsed. Or the first responders can say when the 911 call happened, when they were dispatched, and how long it took them to get there, establishing the time frame for an excited utterance.

Once you have determined the right witnesses to establish an appropriate timeline to invoke the exception, you then must confirm the excitement of the victim. The prosecutor can question the witnesses on the victim's speech, appearance, and behavior to elicit information that portrays the victim as "exited." The victim may have been pacing, waving her hands, speaking rapidly and with a high tone of voice, and crying. While a prosecutor may want to introduce the entirety of a 911 call, do not use the excited utterance exception to overreach. You may have twenty minutes of statements on a 911 tape, but is all of it excited utterances? Also, does the spontaneity of the utterance dwindle as more questions are asked? Only put in the statements that fit squarely under the rule. Do not win the battle only to lose the war on appeal.

Then Existing Mental, Emotional, or Physical Condition

This hearsay exception involves a statement of the declarant's then existing state of mind or emotional, sensory, or physical condition. The statement might reveal the defendant's motive, intention, or plan. The statement might give information about a witness' mental anguish, pain, or physical health. These hearsay exceptions do not include a witness' memory or belief that proves the fact involved, unless it is directly related to the validity of witness' will.

This is an exception that is underutilized, especially in cases of intimate violence. More than ever, people are discussing their mental state and physical conditions. These statements can appear in text messages, conversations, or other forms of communication. A prosecutor can elicit this hearsay exception by asking the right questions. What may be a matter of course to witnesses, like the victim talking about her extreme anxiety, can become relevant in court. Start asking witnesses whether the victim talked about how she felt physically or emotionally. The witnesses may tell you things the victim said like, "My head hurts," "I am devasted he did this again," "I can taste the blood in my mouth," or "I need you to get him out of this house because I am scared." All of these statements reveal the victim's condition.

Statement for the Purpose of Medical Diagnosis and Treatment

Another hearsay exception that includes the victim's statement is for the purpose of medical diagnosis and treatment. This refers to a statement that is made for and pertinent to medical diagnosis and treatment. The statement can describe medical history, past or present symptoms, the inception of the symptoms, or the cause of those symptoms. This is one of the most accepted hearsay exceptions because of the guarantee of trustworthiness. It is believed that if a person is sick or injured, that person is not going to lie to a medical professional, needing treatment for the issue.

It is rather easy to get in statements for medical diagnosis. However, it becomes complicated with Sexual Assault Medical Forensic Exams and Medical Forensic Exams that are done for domestic violence. The defense has been somewhat successful at arguing these statements are testimonial (made in anticipation of litigation) rather than medical because the word "forensic" is used to define the examination. The prosecutor can overcome this by proving that the victim wanted the exam because of medical concerns, not to simply preserve evidence. There are many additional questions the prosecutor can ask of both the victim and the medical provider to establish that the encounter was medical. Some questions the prosecutor may ask include:

- Why was the provider treating the patient? – If the provider claims that the exam was to collect evidence, you will have difficulty convincing the judge that the statements were taken for medical diagnosis and treatment.
- What did the patient believe? – This may offset the medical provider who sees themselves as an evidence collector. If the patient's primary purpose for the exam is a medical concern (e.g., concern about sexually transmitted diseases, pregnancy, injury) that may convince the judge that the patient was there to seek medical treatment.
- What did the informed consent entail? – This question is important for a few reasons. First, it makes the point that consent is always an issue in every healthcare encounter, not just forensic exams. Second, in a forensic exam, there are separate consents for medical treatment and to collect evidence and document injury with photographs. If you can show that the provider would have continued to treat the patient whether the patient wanted evidence collection and/or photographs, you can argue that this was a medical encounter that provided the patient

a courtesy to have a known, empathetic person collect evidence versus sending an evidence technician in to poke, prod, and cause further trauma.

• Why is an assault history important for treatment? – This is a crucial question because it makes the point, much like the questions related to consent, that the treating healthcare provider must always inquire as to what event brought the patient to seek treatment. It guides the examination and allows the provider to concentrate on the areas that need to be treated. You must then ask what symptoms the patient described to elicit testimony about any injuries the patient sustained. These are not questions asked specifically for a forensic exam but are necessary for every healthcare encounter.

There are two other things of note regarding the medical treatment exception. First, the person testifying under this exception does not need to be a doctor or nurse. It is very common to have emergency medical technicians respond to intimate violence crime scenes. EMTs often provide preliminary medical exams and always record what the patient told them, as well as what, if any, treatment they provided. They document this on what is most commonly called the "run sheet." The prosecutor must determine if an ambulance was dispatched and obtain the "run sheet." Not only could it contain key statements of the victim but it is also the discovery that needs to be disclosed. Second, in evidence-based prosecutions, you must sometimes get creative to determine the offender's identity and define the relationship between the victim and offender. The medical exam can be helpful. Who the offender is in cases of interpersonal violence becomes key to any discharge plan. The medical provider must know who the offender is before discharging the patient. The provider needs to determine if the patient requires certain medication in sexual assault cases. If the victim knows the offender, she can advise the provider about what medication might be needed. If the offender is in the victim's home, the provider must decide whether the patient can be discharged to the spouse or partner.

Records of Regularly Conducted Activity (Business Records)

FRE 803 defines a business record as "an act, event, condition, opinion or diagnosis if: The record was made at or near the time by – or from information transmitted by – someone with knowledge." A business record is one kept "in the course of a regularly conducted activity of a uniformed service, business, institution." The record is kept as a regular practice, like a treatment note of a mental health provider, and that who made it was qualified. The creator or another qualified witness can testify to show that the record meets this qualification, or the record can be certified in a way that complies with the rules of evidence. Common business records utilized in intimate violence cases include phone records, leases, credit card statements, cell tower information, utility bills, insurance information, and other records that can provide or corroborate evidence.

911 Calls

Entering 911 calls into evidence poses a particular challenge, but are important in cases when the victim is not participating. The call may be entered as a business record (depending on state law), but the prosecutor must still authenticate the voices on the tape. The call may also be entered as an excited utterance (if the victim called) or statement of a party opponent (if the defendant called). It is possible to enter it as a present sense impression if the event is ongoing and being described on the 911 call. In my experience, it is best to obtain the 902(11) to have but, in addition, subpoena the dispatcher who can testify the name of the person who made the call and authenticate the voice of the person speaking as the person that placed the call that day. If the caller never identified him or herself, you can bring in another witness (family member, co-worker, the responding officers) to identify the caller's voice. Consider putting the victim on the stand to testify that she made the call and the voice on the call is hers, even if she is recanting or minimizing.

Effect on the Listener

First and foremost, the effect on the listener IS NOT an exception to the hearsay rule. Statements that are not offered for the truth of the matter (e.g., only offered to show the effect on the listener or to corroborate the witness's testimony) are not hearsay. Statements that are *not offered for the truth of the matter asserted* do not come in as substantive evidence. The statements can be repeated, but they cannot be argued as evidence. They can still be helpful to the case. For instance, the victim's mother is on the stand, and the prosecutor asks what the victim told her; her response would normally be hearsay. If your response to a hearsay objection is effect on the listener, then what the victim told the mother cannot be considered by the factfinder. It might be essential to elicit that the victim's mother called the police based on what the victim told her, for example. If you want the victim's statement to the mother to come in as substantive evidence so you can argue it in your closing and/ or rebuttal, you must find another exception, such as excited utterance or prior consistent statement.

Prosecutors commonly argue "context" when there is a hearsay objection. This argument reflects the idea that the fact finder needs to hear what was said before or after a statement to put it into proper context. But again, just like the effect on the listener, statements for context cannot be considered substantive evidence. Sometimes the statements that come in for effect on listener or context are just that; it does not matter if they are in evidence. However, if when you analyze the statements, you do want to be able to argue them as substantive, look for another avenue of admissibility. Too often, prosecutors just rely on effect on listener or context as a hearsay response, not realizing what they may be giving up in argument later.

As always in law, there are exceptions to every rule. If you ask the witness a question that will elicit hearsay and the defense does not object, then that statement does come in as substantive. Carefully track when the defense does not object to your questions during trial. However, be aware that this is also true for the defense. Be diligent in objecting to questions that elicit hearsay so that the statements cannot be considered substantively. Be aware that often the defense will ask a question that includes a hearsay response for the purposes of impeachment, which is legally allowed. However, even if it is clear this is what the defense is doing, the prosecution MUST object, forcing the defense to respond that the statement is only for the purposes of impeachment and will not be used as substantive evidence.

Crawford v. Washington, 541 US 36 (2004)

Crawford v. Washington (2004) became a seminal case in the prosecution of intimate violence, much to the chagrin of the prosecution community. The prosecutor's ability to conduct an evidence-based prosecution became incredibly hampered by the Court's opinion in this case, centered around a defendant's Sixth Amendment right to confront the accuser. The Crawford decision and the subsequent cases have been the subject of numerous lengthy law review articles, even books. This discussion of how to proceed with an evidence-based prosecution post-Crawford will not be an in-depth legal analysis, but a practical guide of how to proceed with a prosecution within the limitations Crawford created.

Prior to Crawford, an evidence-based prosecution was relatively straightforward. If a victim chose not to testify and the prosecutor deemed that the defendant needed to be prosecuted, the prosecutor could simply put the first responder on the stand, establish an excited utterance, and obtain testimony on observed injuries. If a 911 tape was available, the prosecutor would call the dispatcher and have it entered as an excited utterance. Crawford changed that for good.

Ironically, the Crawford case did not even involve intimate violence (Crawford v. Washington, 2004). It involved a murder case in the state of Washington where the wife of the defendant, Crawford, initially gave a statement to law enforcement that implicated her husband in a murder. Later at trial, she refused to testify against her husband. The state proceeded to offer her statement into evidence without her testifying. After two state-level appeals, the case found its way to the Supreme Court. The ultimate finding in Crawford was that statements made to law enforcement were "testimonial in nature;" therefore, the defendant had a right to confront the accuser even if a "well-rooted hearsay exception was present." The Supreme Court, however, never defined what the definition of testimonial was, leaving local prosecutors to decipher what that meant. Was a 911 call testimonial? Were statements to the first responding officers testimonial?

The opinions in Davis v. Washington and Hammon v. Indiana gave some answers (2006). These cases were decided in a joint opinion outlined in 126 S. Ct 2266 (2006). It was these cases that defined the word testimonial. Here the Court defined testimonial as statements "made in anticipation of litigation." This was a frustrating and unhelpful definition for domestic violence cases. Most victims of intimate violence do not come to court; it is absurd to suggest that a victim's statements to first responders are in anticipation of prosecution and testifying against the abuser.

Because of the rulings in Davis v. Washington and Hammon v. Indiana (2006), not all statements by first responders are barred. Davis unequivocally states that 911 calls are not testimonial because their primary purpose is to solicit help. Hammon states that generally, statements to first responders are testimonial, unless the prosecution can show that "the emergency was ongoing." For instance, if the offender is not on the scene or the police are trying to determine where the offender is in the house, statements may be non-testimonial statements as the "emergency is ongoing." Prosecutors should not automatically dismiss statements to first responders as barred by Crawford. Additional questions can uncover allowable statements depending on what was happening at the scene.

There are things prosecutors may be able to do to still prosecute evidence-based while complying with the Crawford opinion. For instance, the Crawford opinion does not prohibit the government from calling first responders to testify about an excited utterance that the victim gave to them. It simply states that the defendant has an opportunity to cross-examine the declarant. In intimate partner cases, this is almost always the victim. One best practice is to subpoena the victim and ask just a few questions, even if they are simple factual questions like name, address, or relationship to the offender. Then the prosecution allows the defense to do an unfettered cross-examination. After that, the Confrontation Clause has been satisfied. Now the prosecution is free to call any law enforcement officer who took a statement fitting within a hearsay statement. Other things to consider are to have the victim testify at a preliminary hearing and allow a full cross. This may seem "counterintuitive" to a prosecutor because we constantly worry about impeachment when the victim repeatedly gives a statement. However, it is better to risk a minor impeachment than lose the possibility of being able to present prior testimony at trial.

Forfeiture by Wrongdoing

Although the Supreme Court tied the hands of prosecutors after the Crawford, Hammon, and Davis cases, it gave a glimmer of hope in 2008. In Giles v. California, 554 U.S. 353 (2008), the United States Supreme Court confirmed that the concept of forfeiture by wrongdoing of the Sixth Amendment's right of confrontation remains a powerful tool in prosecuting intimate violence. This decision stood for the concept that if the defendant IS the reason that the victim either cannot or will not testify, the defendant loses the ability to demand the right to confront a witness testifying against him. At the same time, the Court restricted the doctrine requiring that the prosecutor demonstrate the defendant acted with the intent to cause the unavailability of the witness.

The Court recognized that the offender may commit acts of violence against the victim intended to dissuade a victim from resorting to outside help or reporting. This includes acts that attempt to keep the victim from reporting to police and cooperating with the prosecution. The decision acknowledged that even if the offender murdered the victim, there may be evidence that the offender isolated the victim or stopped her from reporting him. If there is evidence that the offender committed acts to interfere with the victim's reporting or cooperation with the prosecution, the victim's prior statements can be admitted under this forfeiture doctrine. This makes it crucial for the prosecutor to uncover earlier abuse or threats of abuse that were meant to discourage the victim's help-seeking, reporting, or testifying.

Forfeiture Hearings with an Uncooperative Victim

How does a prosecutor file a motion and put on evidence in a motion for forfeiture by wrongdoing if the victim is not cooperating? The answer is that hearsay does not apply in motions hearings. You do not need to have the victim testify. The prosecutor can collect and present important information, including the history of abuse, prior charges filed and withdrawn, testimony from the bond hearing, prior cases, and evidence from police, former prosecutor, family, or others about the victim's fear of accused. The motion can contain basically anything to show what the offender did to prevent and/or discourage the victim from testifying.

The prosecutor should work with police to document victim's or other's statements involving:

- The current incident;
- Prior abuse and threats;
- Current/past protection orders;
- Past medical treatment for abuse;
- Past cases related to the abuse (dismissed or not);
- Who the victim told about the abuse;
- Financial dependence on the offender;
- How the victim's behavior changes in the presence of the offender; and
- Any threats the offender made about disclosure or leaving him.

In addition, prosecutors, paralegals, victim witness personnel, and other staff who have contact with victims should be trained to document victim statements during any conversation regarding whether the defendant has acted or made statements to discourage her from testifying. Subpoena or request jail tapes, visitor logs, mail logs – anything to show the defendant's contact with the victim. Call witnesses from different incidents to show the pattern of the abuse and the offender's negative influence on the victim's cooperation with prosecution. Remember that most jurisdictions have a preponderance of the evidence standard for these motions; ensure you check your state laws. An added benefit of filing and winning this type of motion means not just her hearsay statements come into evidence; all her statements come into evidence. Whether these motions are won or not, it is a strong message to the defense and the defendant that the prosecutor will not be intimidated.

Voir Dire Specific to Evidence-Based Cases

Although voir dire has been discussed previously, the prosecutor needs to conduct voir dire differently in an evidence-based prosecution. In evidence-based prosecution, the prosecutor must overcome even more myths and stereotypes and address the fact that the victim is either not present or testifying for the defense. Most importantly, the voir dire questions must be offender-focused. Below are examples of questions the prosecutor can ask:

- If you hear two different versions of events, do you believe that it is possible to be convinced beyond a reasonable doubt?
- If the prosecution can prove the charges beyond a reasonable doubt with other evidence, can you still convict the defendant if the victim does not testify?
- Can you think of reasons why a victim might not want to come to court and testify?
- Would you agree that a victim might not want to testify against their abuser if they feared the abuser?
- Can you think of reasons why a victim might not tell the truth in court?
- Would you agree that a victim might come into court and lie to protect the abuser if they were completely financially dependent on the abuser?
- Do you think that when a victim in a case does not want to proceed, the accused should get a 'free pass"?
- Do you understand that it is the prosecution, not the victim, who decides whether a case is prosecuted?
- Do you think it is a waste of money to prosecute a case where the victim does not want to participate?
- Can you all agree that a victim might not want to participate in a criminal proceeding against their spouse because of X (love, fear, $$)?
- Can anyone think of reasons why the prosecution should go forward if the victim is not participating?
- Can you think of reasons why a victim might not want to testify?
- Can you think of reasons why a victim might say she was not abused when she was?

Although some of the questions ask about the victim and her choices, the idea is to get the jury asking and thinking about how the defendant influenced the victim's choices. You educate the jury, determine who holds bias, and further your theme that the only reason anyone is in court is because of the defendant's actions through voir dire.

Summary

Evidence-based prosecution allows a prosecutor to go forward in their mission for justice less reliant on the victim's participation. While this type of prosecution is extremely useful in cases of domestic or intimate partner violence, it is also very useful in cases where vulnerable victims, like the intellectually disabled, elderly, or non-verbal, have been assaulted. Evidence-based prosecution is not only a legally beneficial strategy but it can also be psychologically beneficial for prosecutors and law enforcement that often suffer the collateral consequences of the offender's reign of terror. In conclusion:

- Domestic and intimate partner violence is lethal and devasting not only to the victims but also to the society at large.
- Evidence-based prosecution should be considered the primary strategy from the onset of any case of intimate violence. This focus ensures that proper evidence is collected in a timely manner to prepare the prosecution in case the victim decides not to cooperate.
- The prosecutor must consider not only the legal and evidentiary aspects of evidence-based prosecution but also the impact of prosecution on the victim as well.
- The prosecutor should understand and utilize all the tools available, including the hearsay exceptions.
- Evidence-based prosecution is the ultimate form of offender-focused prosecution, proving that the offender is the sole target of prosecution.

References

American Academy of Child and Adolescent Psychiatry. (2019). *Domestic violence and children.* AACAP. org. https://www.aacap.org/AACAP/Families_and_Youth/Facts_for_Families/FFF-Guide/Helping-Children-Exposed-to-Domestic-Violence-109.aspx

Bancroft, L., Silverman, J., & Ritchie, D. (2012). *The Batterer as Parent: Addressing the Impact of Domestic Violence on Family Dynamics* (2nd ed.). Sage.

Crawford v. Washington, 541 US 36 (2004). https://supreme.justia.com/cases/federal/us/541/36/

Davis v. Washington, Hammon v. Indiana, 126 S. Ct 2266 (2006). https://wiki.harvard.edu/confluence/display/GNME/Davis+v.+Washington%2C+Hammon+v.+Indiana

Dvorak, P. (2022, October 6). 20 years after the DC Sniper attacks, we keep ignoring what it was all about. *Washington Post.* https://www.washingtonpost.com/dc-md-va/2022/10/06/dc-sniper-mildred-muhammad/

Federal Rules of Evidence. (2020, December 1). https://www.uscourts.gov/sites/default/files/federal_rules_of_evidence_-_december_2020_0.pdf

Geller, L., Booty, M., & Crifasi, C. (2021). The role of domestic violence in fatal mass shooting in the United States, 2014–2019. *Injury Epidemiology, 8*(38). https://injepijournal.biomedcentral.com/articles/10.1186/s40621-021-00330-0

Giles v. California, 554 US 353 (2008). https://supreme.justia.com/cases/federal/us/554/353/

Gwinn, C., & O'Dell, A. (1992). *Stopping the violence: The role of the police officer and the prosecutor.* National Center on Domestic and Sexual Violence. http://www.ncdsv.org/images/stoppingviolence.pdf

Lunnemann, M., Van der Horst, F., Prinzie, P., Luijk, M., & Steketee, M. (2019). The intergenerational impact of trauma and family violence on parents and their children. *Child Abuse & Neglect, 96.* https://doi.org/10.1016/j.chiabu.2019.104134

National Coalition Against Domestic Violence. (n.d.). *Statistics.* Retrieved December 7, 2022, from https://ncadv.org/statistics

National District Attorneys Association. (2009). *National prosecution standards* (3rd ed.). https://ndaa.org/wp-content/uploads/NDAA-NPS-3rd-Ed.-w-Revised-Commentary.pdf

Robinson, C., & Clausen, V. (2021, August 10). *The link between animal cruelty and human violence.* Retrieved December 7, 2022 from https://leb.fbi.gov/articles/featured-articles/the-link-between-animal-cruelty-and-human-violence

Tucker, E. (2022, January 22). *Domestic incidents are highly dangerous for police officers, experts say.* CNN. https://www.cnn.com/2022/01/22/us/domestic-incidents-police-officers-danger/index.html

Willoughby, J. (2017, April 24). Why I stayed. *The Pull of Grace.* http://thepullofgrace.com/journal/2017/4/24/why-i-stayed

Chapter 12

Conclusion

The Real Meaning of Winning

"Really, I'm okay. It doesn't matter now," she said, reassuring the trial team, these authors included. Her perpetrator had been acquitted after drugging and raping her. He had even confessed. She went on to comfort us, probably struck by our confused and apprehensive faces, as we told her the verdict. "They know what he did. I know what he did. You told them. I had a voice," she said. That – her voice – was what she wanted heard by the jury. She did not care about jail. Later that night, the prosecutor got a text with a photo of her beaming smile as she hiked in the quiet woods.

We are concluding our book with examples of how, despite our best efforts, the offender was acquitted. There were many times our team sat in silence after trial, with our drink of choice, wondering, "What the fuck just happened?" We have been stunned and confounded by the jury's or judge's findings. But what we have heard over and over again, despite the acquittal, is that we won. Victims have thanked us for fighting for them, for hearing them, for believing them, and for taking the time to try to understand. It mattered more to the victim that the prosecution team understood her experience more than it mattered that the jury did not. The victims could accept legal issues that impacted the jury's findings as long as they believed the team tried to portray the assault accurately. They have told us they no longer felt alone. The telling of their experience empowered them in and of itself.

Hearing how the victim define winning is how we continue to strive in such a challenging and inhospitable environment for our cause. We have redefined winning. It is not the number of prosecutions that result in convictions that define our success. These cases are too complicated in a world that does not yet value or understand the severity of crimes of intimate violence. Winning is trying when the victim believes there is no hope that anyone would help or hear. Winning is not doing more harm or victimizing the victim again through the process of trial. Winning is bringing empathy and humanity to a cold, dehumanizing process. Winning is being able to point at the offender during the closing to let him know, "we see you."

At the end of each chapter of this book is a summary of important points. We will only use our final chapter to review some of them. The most important point is to remember to approach every case with a determination to understand and reveal the offender to your factfinders, not to defend the victim. Believe that the victim's behaviors are understandable; the victim is acting in a human way through an inhuman experience. You can explain the victim's behaviors, but you never have to apologize for them.

What you are doing matters. We have had direct evidence for years and years. We have successfully prosecuted cases that seemed unwinnable. When juries have been polled after an offender-focused prosecution, the jurors have complimented the prosecutors, saying they finally understood why a victim would go back. After good expert testimony, jurors have reported

DOI: 10.4324/9781003121855-15

that they felt educated and confident in deciding to convict. We have heard court reporters or courtroom staff tell us that they couldn't get that quote from the offender out of their head. Even if the judge does not "get it" this time, you may be able to educate your judge through repeated offender-focused cases.

As an investigator or prosecutor of crimes of intimate violence, you have already taken on the responsibility to become educated and to set your sights on the offender in these cases. Continue to bring curiosity when interviewing victims instead of judgment and blame. In your cases, embrace how extremely complicated intimate violence is and how much we ask of victims. Lift the burden the offender puts on the victim and place it where it belongs, onto the offender. Do this through asking the right questions, offering information, educating the jury, and supporting the resilience and strength of the victims that helped them survive. We can make cases offender-focused. We can expose the offender, stripping away the illusions so he can be seen. We can make a change.

"What did you do to her," the victim's wife asked. She continued as we held our breath, standing devastated after an acquittal based on the judge's ruling for a mistrial. After being brutally raped, the victim threw away her bloody underwear, disgusted by the smell of the rapist they had absorbed. The judge decided that the victim had tampered with evidence, destroying something critical to the case despite the DNA of the offender found in her vagina. "Seriously," the victim's wife continued, "What did you do? She is talking. I saw her smile for the first time in months. She is not scared anymore."

Appendix A

Offender-Focused Interview Questions

Offender-focused interviewing requires different questions and a concentration on information beyond "just the facts, ma'am." The victim is the best source of information about the offender, particularly in an on-going relationship. While it is obviously important to elicit hard facts about the crime and the elements of the crime, it is also important to ask questions that elicit information about the offender and the offender's influence on the victim without insinuating blame, skepticism, or judgment about the victim or the victim's behavior.

A good interviewer can maintain skepticism if information is confusing or seems questionable. But it is entirely useless to broadcast disbelief and skepticism to a victim in the information gathering portion of your contact with your victim. To quell (or confirm) skepticism, it is necessary to get more information, especially if the doubt is couched in a problematic understanding of the victim's behavior, adherence to myths or misinformation, or the interviewer's biased thinking. An interviewer who makes the doubt or disbelief known to the victim can be assured that the victim will provide less information, be more guarded, and be more likely to withdraw from that interview or even cooperation in the case.

One unintentional way to make victims defensive or be less able to provide information is to ask "why" questions. Why didn't you leave? Why didn't you scream? Why did you drink so much? All of these questions are *victim*-focused, not offender-focused. The victims' answers are less likely to be helpful, more likely to be vague, or require answers the victim does not know. Remember, victims are viewing themselves in hindsight, focused on what they could have done differently to have prevented being assaulted. Questions about "why" they did what they did trigger no consideration or insight that will be helpful to the case. The most likely response to "why" is "I don't know," because the victims themselves cannot come up with explanations given the ultimate outcome.

Offender-focused interviewing not only reveals more information but it also keeps the information focused on the offenders – how they manipulated and influenced the situations, as well as placed the victim in the position to have to make choices in the first place. The following list has been adapted and supplemented from an original list by this author (Valliere, 2019).

Question Format

Avoiding the "why" question can be difficult. It takes practice. Better phrases to use include:

- How did … (you decide to, that happen, he make you)
- What made you … (freeze, get in his car, submit)
- What were you thinking/was going through you mind when …

- What did the offender do to … (gain your trust, make you forgive him, get you back)
- What were you feeling when …
- What was it like when …
- Tell me about when/what/how …
- Explain more about that …
- Help me understand …

Offender-Focused Questions to Explore Offender Influence

- What did he do to keep you from telling?
- How did he help you get over it? Forgive him?
- What did he do to get you to come back? Trust him again?
- What did he do/how did he act after the assault? How did that affect you?
- What did you love about him? How did it change over time?
- What excuses or rationalizations did he make for his behavior?
- Did he ever do things to try to confuse you about what happened?
- What did he do to make you trust him?
- You told him (sent him photos/sent him texts/had sex with him) after the assault. What made you choose to do that? What did he do that helped you make that decision?
- Did he ever apologize, ask for forgiveness, promise to get help? How did that impact your decisions?
- What experience do you have trying to resist or fight with him? What does he do?
- What would usually happen between you after an assault?
- Before he raped you, did you have any reason to think he would do something like this?
- How does he present in public versus private?
- Tell me about the first time he did something you had to forgive or forget. How did he make it up to you? Blame you for it?
- What did he say to make you think this was your fault? How about before this? What did he say to make you think you brought stuff on yourself? (*pushed my buttons, make me jealous, you know how I am, you are crazy*)
- What has he done when you have tried to leave/break up before?
- What does he do to make you feel helpless?
- Has there ever been anything you could do to calm him down or make things good again? (*pleasing, make up sex, pretending it didn't happen*) If you did these things, how did it get better for you?
- What kinds of things does he tell other people about you?
- Has he ever put you in a situation where you confronted him in public?
- Has he ever said people wouldn't believe you or otherwise made you doubt your support? Has he proven it to you?
- How has he threatened or intimidated you in the past?
- What did he do during the time before the assault to make you feel safe? Confuse you? Isolate you? Increase your vulnerability/intoxication?
- What does he know about you that he has used against you?
- Are there other ways he has threatened, intimidated, or controlled you?
- Does he know things about you that he hurts you with or that you are afraid others will find out?
- How does he act around other people? Does your family like him?

- Is it hard to believe he would do something like this? How come?
- Has he ever used the children against you? Tell me about that.
- Has he ever turned others against you? How has he done that?
- Has he ever limited your access to others?
- Does he have access to your social media? Passwords?
- What will he be telling others about you? Is there something he is saying to his attorney about you or that event that we should know?
- Do you feel like you are safe? If not, tell me about that. Does he have weapons?

Exploring Victim Decision-Making or Responses

- What made you decide not to ... scream, leave, run?
- When did you decide that it was okay to stay or that the danger was over? How did you decide that?
- When did you believe it was safe? What made you think that?
- When the assault started, what did you think was happening?
- What kept you from escaping, texting for help?
- You told him you loved him/sent him photos/sent him texts/had sex with him after. What made you choose to do that?
- What made you think that kissing him/having sex/not screaming was a good idea at the time?
- How did you try to resist? Had this worked for you in the past with people?
- Tell me about your personality and how you related to people. How do your choices fit with your personality? *(I am not violent; I wanted to stay to protect my friend; I don't like causing problems; I am a Christian/forgiving/taught to give people a second chance)*
- What decisions did you make to try to deal with him?
- What were you feeling after? Tell me what you were thinking the next day.
- Were you worried about anything during the assault, like getting pregnant or the kids seeing you? Tell me about it.
- Did anything strange happen to you, like you felt like leaving your body or something else?
- How did you try to help it be over?
- How did you cope when it was happening? How about after it was over?
- What questions do you think people have about how you acted?
- Do you blame yourself? How come?
- What have you learned from your family on how to deal with these things? Your religion? Your culture? The offender?
- How do you think other people will view this? Did this affect your decisions in any way?
- What things kept you from leaving?
- Have you ever tried to leave/resist before? What happened?

Getting information from a position of curiosity, as opposed to analysis and judgment, is an effective stance to adopt, regardless of what you might believe or think internally. This method of interviewing can help you address even the most difficult questions in your interview. Remember, too, that how you structure your direct conveys the beliefs and attitudes you want the fact finders to adopt. If you elicit information in an "of course it makes sense manner," that will be transmitted to the jury. Do not avoid the issues you find challenging. If the victim is able to address any issue on direct, it neutralizes any "surprise" attack on cross and minimize any perception that the prosecution is trying to hide information. Most importantly, the case remains focused on the offender.

Reference

Valliere, V. (2019). *Understanding victims of interpersonal violence: A guide for investigators and prosecutors.* Routledge Press.

Sample Voir Dire Questions

Voir dire is a key place to begin addressing myths, biases, and misinformation about intimate violence. Below are some sample areas to consider formulating questions around to address with your jury/panels. Rules of voir dire differ depending on the judge or jurisdiction in which you practice. Consider the content area for what you can personally address in your own courtroom.

Addressing Myths about Intimate Violence

- Intimate crimes are private.
- The majority of intimate crimes are committed by loved ones or people known to the victim.
- There are usually no witnesses to any type of crime.
- People can love someone even if they are hurt by them.
- Intimate crimes are sometimes considered "family" or marital problems; it might be hard for a victim to realize they are crimes.
- Offenders can make excuses for their behaviors or promise it will never happen again.
- It is hard to admit someone we love can hurt us.
- Even if someone is intoxicated, they can still be raped.
- It is important to have consent for sexual contact.
- It is still a crime to assault someone even if it happens in a family.
- There is nothing that someone can do to deserve to be raped/battered.
- Everyone responds differently to a traumatic event.
- There is no typical way an offender/victim looks or acts in public.

Addressing Myths about Victim Behavior

- It is very embarrassing to report very intimate or sexual details to strangers.
- Someone might not be ready to report abuse right away.
- A spouse might want to try to work on a marriage, even if the other spouse is abusive.
- People can blame themselves for bad things or be afraid other people will blame them.
- Sometimes telling about abuse takes a long time, even years.
- People can forgive even very bad things for a long time until they decide not to anymore.
- Someone who is being assaulted could decide to submit so they are not hurt worse or to get it over with sooner.
- People can be terrified of being abandoned, poor, family-less.
- It is very hard to leave a marriage.
- There may be very practical reasons not to leave a relationship, even if it is abusive.

- There may be religious or cultural factors that affect someone's behavior.
- Hoping someone will change, especially if they promise to, can affect decisions.
- Sometimes it is easier to talk about terrible things when you feel safe, like when the person who hurts you is gone.
- People can be threatened into keeping secrets.

Addressing Memory Issues or "Consistency"

- People do not tell the same story the same way each time.
- When people are feeling strong emotions, details may get confused, but not the main event.
- What someone asks or how they ask it can affect someone's answer.
- Embarrassment, fear, and shame can impact how someone relays an event.
- Someone might remember different things at different times.
- Memories or details can be triggered or come back to someone later.
- That just because someone doesn't say something exactly the same way every time it doesn't mean they are lying.

Offender Behavior

- Sexual abuse is so unbelievable that people chose to deny it.
- Offenders commit crimes in private, with no witnesses.
- Even if people have some good traits, they can have some very bad traits.
- People can seem one way in public but be completely different in private.
- People can be good at their jobs or have a good reputation and still hurt people.
- There is no physical evidence related to being kissed, touched, rubbed, licked, tickled, or having to watch things.
- Offenders are always responsible for committing a crime, even if they are angry.
- It is not a crime to love someone; it is a crime to rape someone.
- Offenders should be held accountable even if someone "doesn't tell."
- Alcohol does not cause you to be sexually attracted to children.
- Sometimes people abuse their power or rank.
- Having status gives people some power to get away with things.
- No one can make someone rape them.
- You cannot tell who is a rapist or abuser by the way they look.

This is only a sampling of the concepts to address in voir dire. Become familiar with general myths and misinformation about intimate violence, victims, and offenders. Address the issues you perceive will be brought up in the case. Introduce the offender-focused theme through your voir dire.

Appendix C

Sample Chapters for Sexual Assault and Intimate Partner Violence Cases

Below are sample outlines for a direct of a victim in a sexual assault case and a case of domestic violence. The outline offers areas to explore and sample questions to elicit the relevant offense information and evidence in the victim's testimony. These are only samples based on hypothetical cases to exemplify an offender-focused direct; they should be modified to fit your specific case.

Chapters – Sexual Assault – Alcohol-Facilitated Acquaintance Rape

- Victim's History and Family

    - Where did you grow up?
    - How long did you live in XX?
    - Tell the Jury about your family.

- Victim's education

    - High school – How big? Involved in activities?
    - College – Where? Degree attained?

- Victim's career
- Social life

    - Social person?
    - Enjoy large get-togethers?
    - Smaller get-togethers?
    - What do you like to do on the weekends?

- Drinking history

    - What is your experience drinking?
    - What do you normally drink?

- Drinking before assault

    - Where?
    - How much?
    - With whom?

- Meeting the Accused

  - Where?
  - How?
  - Who else was there? Did he know your friends?
  - What was your first impression? What did friends say about him?

- Conversation with the Accused

  - What did he say to you?
  - What did you say to him?
  - How did he interact with you? Was he likeable?
  - Was there anything he did to make him seem dangerous or a threat?

- Leaving with the Accused

  - Whose idea was it to leave?
  - How did you leave? Did you have a car?
  - How were you feeling?
  - Who decided where to go?

- In the Accused's Apartment

  - Explain the layout of room with picture
  - What did he do when you first got there?
  - Did you know where you were or how to get home?
  - Where did you first sit?
  - Where did he first sit?
  - Did he offer you anything? Food? Alcohol?
  - What made you move to the bed?
  - What did you think was going to happen?
  - When did you realize he wasn't really interested in watching a movie?

- Sexual assault

  - Where did he first touch you?
  - What did you do to let him know you weren't interested?
  - What was his response?
  - What were you thinking when he grabbed you by the hair?
  - What did he do after he grabbed you by the hair?
  - How did you decide to cope with the assault in that moment?
  - Check elements.

- Immediately after the Assault

  - What did he say after he ejaculated?
  - Were you able to say anything back?
  - What stopped you from leaving right away?
  - When did you feel safe to leave?
  - Did he do anything to keep you there?

- Leaving after the assault

    - How did you get home?
    - Did you talk to anyone about the assault after?
    - What made you not want to call the police?
    - What did you do when you got home?

- The Aftermath

    - Did you ever hear from him?
    - What was going through your mind the next day?
    - How did you decide what to do about reporting the assault?

Chapters – Intimate Partner Violence Case

- Victim's History and Family (as above)
- Victim's Education (as above)
- Victim's Career

    - What/how long?
    - How much responsibility?
    - Where does the money go?

- Victim's LACK of Career/job

    - When did you stop working?
    - Whose idea was that? How was that decision made?
    - Who is the primary provider in the family?
    - Did you work before meeting the accused?

- How they met

    - When
    - Where
    - How

- The beginning of the relationship

    - First Date
    - What did you like about him?
    - What things did he do to build your love and trust?
    - Favorite things to do; Dreams you started building
    - Timeline
    - Emotions

- Engagement

    - How quickly did you become engaged?
    - Were you ready for this?
    - How long did the engagement last?
    - What made you decide to marry him?

- Marriage

    - What was that day like?
    - How long were things good?
    - What were the rules or expectations of your marriage?

        - Children
        - Finances
        - Friends
        - Family
        - Religion

- WHAT CHANGED?

    - Did he begin speaking to your differently? How so?
    - Did he begin to change his expectations? How so?
    - What did he do to first make you feel uncomfortable or upset in the relationship?

- First assault

    - What happened (hit the elements)?
    - What was going through your mind when he (hit, kicked, punched) you?
    - Was there a reason you didn't tell people what he did?
    - Were you able to seek medical treatment?
    - Did he do anything to make sure you did not tell?
    - What made you not want to call the police?
    - What if anything did he say afterwards?
    - Did he do anything to show he was sorry (apologies, flowers, cards)?
    - Did he promise you anything?
    - What made you stay?

- Environment after the assault

    - How long was it calm?
    - Did he keep some of his promises? For how long?
    - Did he do anything to confuse you about the assault? Blame you?
    - (Do not be afraid to elicit any positive information that will help make sense of the victim's desire to stay or protect the offender.)

- Second assault

    - What happened (hit the elements)?
    - (Revisit versions of the same questions asked about the first assault.)
    - Tell me more about your reaction to him abusing you again.
    - What options did you have?
    - Did he do anything to try to make you stay? Forgive him? Trust him again?

- Leaving

    - What made you decide to leave?
    - Ask allowable questions about the offender's reaction to the victim's leaving.

        - Pleading, begging
        - Sending messages through the children

- Reconciliations

    - Explore the process and offender's behavior that instigated the reconciliations.
    - Explore the struggles that the victim faced after leaving.

- Divorce
- Custody
- Revealing the abuse

    - What triggered the disclosure?
    - Ask questions to show the absence of any motive to lie.

- Lies told by the offender

    - Ask questions regarding any retaliation or lies the offender has told.
    - Ask questions about whether the offender is manipulating family or children.

Appendix D

Samples of the Use of Technology at Trial

Providing visual representations of the evidence through the use of technology can be powerfully influential to the fact finders. Projecting photos of the victim who was much younger can highlight the vulnerability or reality of the victim, especially if the victim is older when the trial occurs. Juxtaposing the victim's statements with the offender's statements can spotlight evidence that could get lost, highlighting points that might otherwise be too subtle. Below are some sample slides with examples from cases that were presented as a PowerPoint to the jury.

It can be very useful to have a slide that shows each element of a crime linked to the corresponding element. Like the slide above, columns can be used, with "Elements" on the left and "Evidence" on the right. Each bullet on the left describing the element can have corresponding bullets on the right, indicating to the jury where evidence of the element was provided (Figure APPD.1).

Reminding juries what reasonable doubt is can be very helpful. A slide with the legal definition of reasonable doubt, specifically with the verbiage outlining that reasonable doubt is not "fanciful" or conjecture and that it does not exclude every possibility, followed by a slide like the one below, can capture your version of the facts as to what is reasonable and unreasonable (Figure APPD.2).

Credibility: Consistent vs. Inconsistent

- Victim
  - To sister: "My best friend raped me."
  - To nurse: "My best friend raped me."
  - To law enforcement: "I drank with my friend and woke up with him on top of me, inside me."
  - During the preliminary hearing: "I threw up in the sink and went to sleep on the floor. The next thing I remember I was on the bed and he was inside of me"

- The Accused
  - "We had dinner, watched a movie, that's it."
  - "Well, I tried to have sex with her but I couldn't get it up."
  - "Nothing happened."
  - "Yes, we had sex but it was consensual."
  - "We had rough sex."

Figure APPD.1 Corroborating Credibility.

Interpretation of Facts: Reasonable Doubt

ACTION	REASONABLE	UNREASONABLE
Victim drinks several hard alcohol drinks in 2 hours and vomits in the sink	Victim is highly intoxicated	*Accused didn't know she was intoxicated*
Victim goes to sleep on the floor fully clothed	Victim is so intoxicated, she couldn't get to the bed 3 feet away	*Victim was just napping before the awesome consensual sex*
Victim says no, but accused continues to penetrate her	Victim did not want to have sex with the accused	*She didn't really mean 'no.'*
Accused's story evolves every time he gets a new piece of information	Accused is lying to stay out of trouble.	*The accused was trying to protect the victim's reputation.*

Figure APPD.2 Combating Reasonable Doubt.

Slides with graphic displays of a timeline can make visual all the offender's criminal actions, showing what overlapped, what happened quickly, and what behaviors persisted. It can also provide a graphic representation of the duration of the offender's behavior, especially if the charged offenses only reflect a single moment in time.

Photos can be utilized very effectively in a presentation to the jury. A photo of injury can underlie a list of the offender's statements about them. For instance, a photo of the victim's bruised back with the offender's denials splayed on top of it can give a dramatic image for the jury. The offender might have said, "I didn't hit her," "I hugged her too tight," "Maybe she did it to herself," "She lies," or "Sometimes she wants to be hit." Image those phrases over stomp marks on a victim. Another photo array demonstrating the "changing faces of the accused" could show images of the poor behavior of the accused the night of the crime in contrast with professional photo shot.

The use of slides to compare and contrast evidence can be dramatic. The same slides can compare and contrast the prosecution versus the defense arguments, the parties' motives to fabricate, or what makes the victim versus the accused credible. Slides can remind the jury of impactful information or events that happened during trial. By providing information both visually and auditorily, the jury has multiple avenues to access memory of your case when the jury is in the deliberation room.

Sentencing Questions for Victims

If a prosecutor can conceptualize the impact and damage from intimate violence as rippling or radiating, the questions for a sentencing interview or eliciting testimony can encompass a much broader scope, conveying a more comprehensive account of the impact of the assault to the fact finders. Exploration of the effects of the crime and the scope of the trauma can be structured from a micro-view to a macro-view. This guide has been adapted from a previously published work (Valliere, 2019), with additions and modifications.

This image presumes that the victim is a woman. Modify the concept to fit the victim you are working with during sentencing. Think of the victim interview like this (see Figure APPE.1):

1 **Self** – Probe the impact on the person's individual identity –

a Thoughts about self –

   i Damaged
  ii Stupid
 iii Ashamed, embarrassed
 iv Weak, vulnerable
  v Uncertain about decisions, choices, judgments

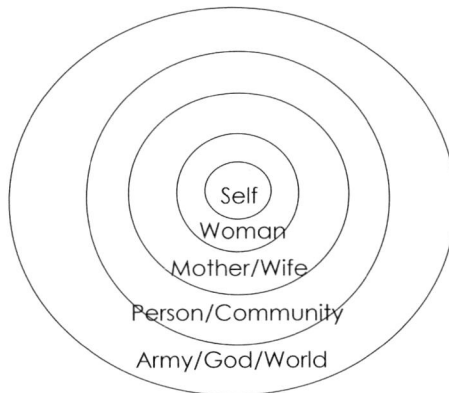

Figure APPE.1 Areas for Exploration.

b   What are some of the symptoms you struggle with now?

    i Sleep or appetite problems – nightmares, fear, diarrhea
    ii Emotional changes – Anxiety, depression, irritability, numbing
    iii Loss of joy, trust
    iv Social withdrawal
    v Nightmares, hypervigilance, hyperarousal
    vi Efforts to avoid all reminders, triggers, places
    vii Concentration, attention, learning problems

c   How has this affected your sense of self-worth, value, or lovability?
d   Physical health or injury from the assault

2   **Changes in Self as an Intimate/Sexual Being** – Explore changes in the victim sense of sexuality or intimacy

a   Did this affect your sexuality?
b   Do you have any feelings of disgust or shame about sex? Your body?
c   Did it impact your ability to trust? Be close to others? Be in love again?

3   **Partner/Lover/Parent** – Explore changes in intimate relationships

a   How did this affect your relationship with your lover/spouse?
b   How has it affected your parenting? Your relationship with your children?
c   Can you be vulnerable in your relationships?
d   Are your habits with your family changed? (don't go out, don't sleep with, overprotective of the children, won't go places with the family)
e   Do you have issues with depression, anger, irritability that impact your family?
f   Have you lost your sense of competency or desirability as a mate?
g   Are some of your trauma symptoms drawing you away from others (not able to be hugged by children)?
h   How has this affected your ability to bond with or care for your children?
i   How has this impacted the dynamics in your family?

4   **Person/Community/Friend/Family/Work**

a   Has this rape/assault changed the way you interact with others?
b   Is it as easy to be someone's friend?
c   Did you get support from others?
d   Did you withdraw? Did you lose friends from this?
e   Has this changed the way you deal with strangers?
f   Are you different when you are around others?
g   Did you get any retaliation from other people?
h   Has your work/school/suffered?
i   Has it affected your sense of competence at work or school?

5   **God/Military/Community/World View**

   a   Has your relationship with God or your faith been affected?

   b   Has this changed the way you think of the world? How?

   c   How has this changed your perception of other people?

Using directive questions, you can guide the victim to consider things other than just the immediate impact of injury or the associated losses that victims more easily identify. Victims struggle with understanding the impact of the crime; you can help with a more comprehensive interview.

Reference

Valliere, V. (2019). *Understanding victims of interpersonal violence: A guide for investigators and prosecutors.* Routledge Press.

Index

abuse 12, 22–26, 33, 35–38, 40–42, 51, 56, 64, 67, 104, 111
abuser 11, 12, 18–20, 22, 24, 34, 35, 54–56, 100, 101, 112
acute mental illness 20, 28
adequacy issues 21–22
aggression 20–24, 36, 104
alcohol 12, 19, 20, 28, 37, 73, 80, 121, 123; myopia 20; use 12, 19–20, 37
American Psychiatric Association 32
anger management problems 21–22
antisocial traits 22–24
attrition 13

bad acts 64, 70, 75, 76; evidence 69, 70
base-rate fallacy 9–10
battering 7, 19
beliefs 6, 9, 10, 20–24, 49, 50, 80, 82, 84
biases 5–10, 13, 14, 27, 49, 50, 58, 59, 79, 80; binary bias 8–9; confirmation bias 6; definition 6; halo effect 7–8; hindsight bias 6–7; investigation and prosecution 6
binary bias 8–9
binary thinking *see* binary bias
boldness 21
Bugliosi, Vince 86

case, building 49–52; challenges, questions and assumptions 50–51; charging decisions 51; follow-up 50; foundation 50; missing information 50–51; myths, impact 49–50; paradigm shift 49
children 2, 25, 35, 38, 40, 41, 80, 101–103, 106, 125, 126, 130; molesters 19; victims 12, 54
cognition 32–33
confirmation bias 6
confusion 36–37
conviction 11, 14, 102–104, 114
counterintuitive behaviors 42, 64, 68, 69
criminal justice system 11; bias, myth acceptance, and misinformation 13–14; jury decision-making 14;

law enforcement and investigation 13; negative experience 39–40; protection of others 40
"cry rape" 9
culture 36

Daubert v. Merrell Dow Pharmaceuticals, Inc., 509 U.S. 579 (1993) 94
decision-making 6, 14, 32–34
defendants, attractiveness 7–8
defense theme 71, 72
denial 36–37
"devil" effect 8
disbelief 36–37
domestic violence 7, 95; cases 5, 100, 103, 110; "no-drop" policies 5; offenders 21, 101, 102; prosecution of 5

emotion of fear 34, 35
empathy 1, 21–24, 41, 57–58, 114
entitlement 21–24, 104
Epstein, D. 9
evidence-based prosecution 100–113; charging decisions, basis 103; Crawford v. Washington, 541 US 36 (2004) 109–110; decide whether to proceed with 102; excited utterance 106; forfeiture, wrongdoing 111; forfeiture hearings, uncooperative victim 111–112; listener, effect 109; medical diagnosis and treatment 107–108; mental, emotional, or physical condition 107; 911 calls 108–109; present sense impression 106; produce the victim 102–103; prosecuted, offender 103–105; regularly conducted activity records (business records) 108; victim's statements, admissibility 105–106; voir dire 112; work with law enforcement 105
expert 76, 84, 85, 90, 91, 94–96, 99; testimony 94–96; witness 1
exploitiveness 24
external factors 38; access to services/assistance 38–39; societal response and rejection 39
extra-legal factors 10